Dust to Dust

In the VISUAL STUDIES series, edited by Douglas Harper

Ronald Silvers, *A Pause on the Path* (1988)

Builder Levy, *Images of Appalachian Coalfields* (1989)

Richard Quinney, *Journey to a Far Place: Autobiographical Reflections* (1991)

Glenn Busch, *You Are My Darling Zita* (1991)

Melody D. Davis, *The Male Nude in Contemporary Photography* (1991)

Charles Keil, Angeliki V. Keil, and Dick Blau, *Polka Happiness* (1992)

A DOCTOR'S
VIEW OF
FAMINE IN
AFRICA

David Heiden

Dust to Dust

Temple University Press

Philadelphia

Temple University Press, Philadelphia 19122
Copyright © 1992 by Temple University
All rights reserved. Published 1992
Printed in Canada

Library of Congress
Cataloging-in-Publication Data
Heiden, David.
Dust to dust : a doctor's view of famine in
Africa / David Heiden.
p.   cm. — (Visual studies)
ISBN 0-87722-912-0
1. Famines—Sudan—Case studies.
2. Famines—Sudan—Pictorial works.
I. Title.   II. Series.
HV630.H45   1992
363.8'09624—dc20
91-37247

This book is dedicated

to my parents,

Herbert and Natalin Heiden,

and to my wife,

Katherine Seligman

CONTENTS

ACKNOWLEDGMENTS

This book has taken five years, and although my name appears alone on the cover, it never would have happened without help from many people.

I initially conceived of this project as a picture story. Many people, but particularly Bill Jay and Bruce Davidson, finally convinced me that I needed to write what happened. Nevertheless, the photos have been the part most alive to me. I'm indebted to many photographers who generously reviewed proof sheets, work prints, slides, or other forms of the work: Katy Raddatz, Nick Nichols, Chris Killup, Arnold Newman, Linda Conner, Ken Light, Mary Ellen Mark, Michele Vignes, Naomi Weissman, Janet Delaney, Doug Menuez, Eugene Richards, Lois Conner, Fred Woodward, Matt Mahurin, Mike Rosen, Fred Richin, John Issacs, Abigail Heyman, Bedrich Grunzweig, Ruth Lester, Sandra Eisert, Stu Levy, Takeshi Yuzawa, Debra Heimerdinger, Jane Heiden, William Klein, and Kim Komenich. Book prints were made by Amy Whiteside, Tim Burman, and Eddie Dyba; maps by Lori Lietzke.

Carole Kismaric, Michael Kenna, and Gilles Peress have influenced how I understand my own photographs and how I have used them in shaping a story and composing a book. Michael has helped with everything from sequencing images to spotting prints.

The writing and rewriting was the most formidable part, and I'm grateful to those who read different chapters and editions: Steve Gomer, Nan Richardson, Claire Peeps, Raymond Lifchez, Judith Stronach, Jack Schapiro, William Parmer,

x

ACKNOWLEDGMENTS

Steve Heiden, Jeffrey Schneider, Martha Ryan, Ian Timm, Barbara Smith, and Bruce Buschel. My wife, Katherine Seligman, edited every draft and encouraged me for five years.

My entire family encouraged my work with refugees, particularly my parents, who often provided the financial support that made it possible.

Jan Ralph, at the United Nations, and Jim Breetveld and Peter David, at UNICEF, have been generous with encouragement and support. Without their help my photo work would have been impossible. The International Rescue Committee (IRC) sent me to Sudan, and later Robert DeVecchi graciously allowed me to review the IRC records. Bruce Ostler made it possible for me to return to Sudan, then accompanied me there and encouraged me in pursuing this work.

I wish to thank my co-workers in Sudan. I have high regard for what they brought to their jobs and what it cost them. I regret if this book causes any of them pain. To protect their privacy I have changed the names.

In presenting this account I'm aware it is a highly personal record, not objective history. Others may remember things differently. I record things here based on who I am: someone who is judgmental and critical; impatient and sometimes angry at my own limitations, and, unfortunately, also at the human failings of my colleagues. Despite the problems we faced and the mistakes we made, our relief work was valuable. Such work should be continued.

Finally, I thank the refugees, who will probably never see their pictures or read what an outsider perceived of their tragedy. Perhaps their children or grandchildren will come across this or some other record of 1985, and it will have meaning.

Dust to Dust

Prologue

A WORLD AWAY

In the spring of 1985, I left my home in San Francisco to work in the refugee camps of eastern Sudan. It was an experience that often overwhelmed me and now occupies the space of years in my memory and in my life. I knew I was having an experience with far more in it than I could live as it happened.

I kept a diary, and I compulsively took photographs. The pictures are about refugees, but the story is really about Western relief workers. It is a story about confronting and attempting to remedy a set of circumstances that were far beyond our comprehension or control. It is a story about how we became part of the disaster we were sent to contain.

It took me six months to regain my emotional equilibrium after I left Sudan. It was a year before I could begin serious work on this book, and now, after five years, piles of text and photographs still litter my home.

When I first got back, people would ask me, "How was Africa? What was it like in the Sudan?" I got into the habit of saying, "It was a great place to get a tan and lose weight" and then direct the conversation away. Sometimes when I started to answer truthfully, I could see people get uneasy, frightened by my intensity or by the horrifying things I described. The experience was too complex, with too many euphoric moments and too much pain. I couldn't figure out a simple way to tell it.

After living in an African famine, restaurants were like a fantasy world. Each menu was a paralyzing, overwhelming choice. And I had trouble about food in other ways. It still bothers me to see anything left on a table. When I first got back, I would take home the leftover bread, along with any of the dishes that I, or even a companion, didn't finish. One day I actually tried to take home the butter.

For several months I was unable to look at my photos. Then I became obsessed. I went into the darkroom and made print after print, more than a thousand work prints, driven to find something that could not be found in any photograph. Maybe it was a first attempt to control on paper an experience I could not control in any other way. During those hours in the darkroom I used a tape deck to hear books, and I listened to the

entire reading of Winston Churchill's six-volume *History of the Second World War*. Then I listened to Daniel Defoe's *Journal of the Plague Year*, a book of personal observations about a pestilence that happened in 1665.

Ivory Tower in a Jungle

The trip to Sudan was not the first time I'd worked in refugee camps or in Africa. I began by chance. In December 1979, a friend passed through the emergency room where I worked and asked if I wanted to go to Thailand to help the Cambodian refugees. It had not occurred to me before. I didn't know the difference between Lon Nol and Pol Pot. But I immediately knew that I wanted to go.

I had been a history major in college and had keenly followed world events. In the intervening years, in the process of learning medicine, I had lost touch. I was marking time in the emergency room, with a vague sense that it was time I started making a lot of money. The only decision I faced was choosing a ski cabin for the coming winter. I told myself that six intense weeks of charity work in Asia would burn off a dissatisfaction I could feel but was unable to understand. I also saw the trip as a chance for free travel, an adventure following which, I assumed, a career direction would emerge. After several false starts, in April 1980 I found myself working on a ward at Khao I Dang refugee camp on the Thai-Cambodian border.

Then, in the winter of 1981–82, I made another overseas trip, this time to Somalia. I first thought about working there while jogging in Golden Gate Park in the rain, trying to heal a failed romance. Africa frightened me. In the midst of planning the trip, I woke up one night from a horrible dream about being in a desolate place and having to sleep in the sand. But my second trip, as expatriate medical director of Boo'co refugee camp, was more fascinating and rewarding than the first.

By the time I thought about a third trip, I had become acting medical director of the emergency room where I worked. I was encouraged to take the full-time post as director, but was ambivalent. I finally decided not to take the job. In May 1983 I went to Uganda to work on an emergency immunization campaign.

So I arrived in Sudan with some experience. I also arrived with strong opinions. For example, I thought that setting up hospitals in refugee camps was a mistake. I had thought the opposite in 1980, on the Thai-Cambodian border, where another doctor and I managed a seventy-bed hospital ward, in a gravel-floored shack made of thatch, bamboo, and blue plastic sheeting. We worked in a style reminiscent of an American intensive care unit, in the middle of a rice field, with sounds of artillery fire in the distance. It was exciting. With only one day off in a six-week stint, I was too busy to give a thought to what would happen when I, and the rest like me, had to leave. It was "ivory tower" medicine in a jungle, and since there were doctors stepping all over themselves to take care of the Cambodian refugees, I never perceived how incongruous it all was in relation to overall health needs or to what could be afforded and sustained.

In Somalia, in 1981, I was at first shocked to discover that the policymakers in the Somali Refugee Health Unit had forbidden refugee-camp hospitals. They were shrewd leaders and taught us to spend much of our time teaching. All health measures emphasized the importance of sanitation and decent food and water. I learned the fundamental priorities for a refugee-camp doctor. Still, I was not prepared for Sudan.

Civil War and Famine

It's hard to comprehend why, in a world with adequate food, the African famine of 1984–85 occurred. Events in Ethiopia took place against a background of failed development policies for all of sub-Saharan Africa, where Western governments, for their own financial advantage, and World Bank policies encouraged planting cash crops instead of food. In Ethiopia the crowded central highlands of Tigre province suffered years of deforestation and soil erosion. Feudal landlords during decades of Haile Selassie's rule drained surplus wealth with little reinvestment in the rural infrastructure. Then, by 1984, there had been several years of severe drought.

Political conflicts, lunacy, and civil war turned this crisis into immeasurable disaster. By way of engaging proxies to fight cold war battles, the United States and the Soviet Union had heavily armed numerous factions in the Horn of Africa, fueling conflicts in a historically unstable region. In September 1984 the Ethiopian president, Haile Mariam Mengistu, spent an estimated $100 million to celebrate the tenth anniversary of his revolution, while in the countryside his population starved. Well after reliable famine information came out, the Reagan administration remained locked in internal squabbles, reluctant to help a Marxist regime.

Two northern Ethiopian provinces, Tigre and Eritria, were fighting a civil war with the central government, the Dergue of President Mengistu. By late 1984 most of Tigre was controlled by the Tigre Peoples Liberation Forces and their civil/humanitarian counterpart, the Relief Society of Tigre (REST).

Confronting starvation, peasant farmers in Tigre had two choices about where to seek help: They could look to the government or flee to Sudan. Many went to government-controlled cities to seek famine relief from the Dergue, which used the assistance to their political advantage. Sometimes peasants who were not members of government-sponsored associations were refused food. Relief food was stolen by the government and used to pay their soldiers; in government towns, the peasants risked conscription into the army or forced relocation from their land and resettlement in the south.

The other choice was to seek refuge in Sudan. In the six months between November 1984 and April 1985, REST led ap-

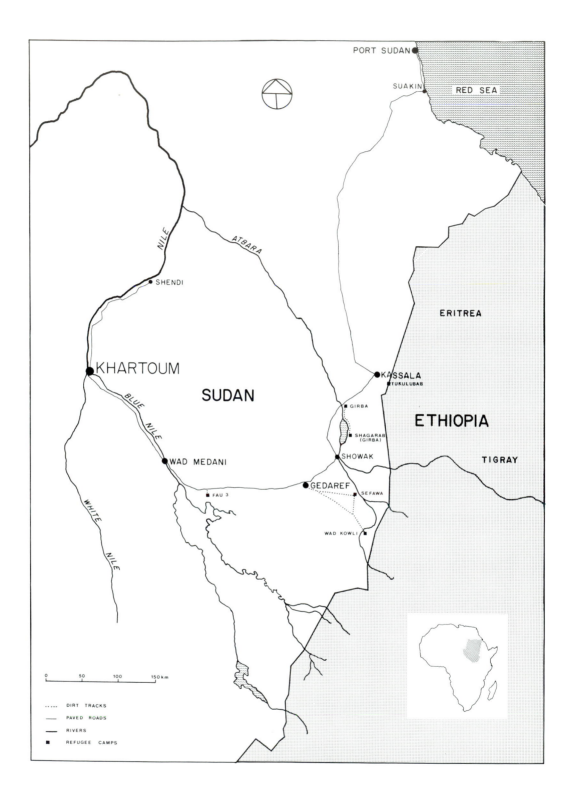

PORT SUDAN

SUAKIN   RED SEA

NILE

ATBARA

● SHENDI

KHARTOUM

SUDAN

● KASSALA
■ TUKULUBAB

■ GIRBA

BLUE NILE

ETHIOPIA

■ SHAGARAB
(GIRBA)

● WAD MEDANI

SHOWAK

TIGRAY

■ FAU 3

●GEDAREF

■ SEFAWA

WHITE NILE

WAD KOWLI ■

ERITREA

0   50   100   150 km

⋯⋯   DIRT TRACKS

───   PAVED ROADS

━━━   RIVERS

■   REFUGEE CAMPS

proximately 170,000 people in a three-week journey on foot from Tigre into Sudan. They crossed steep mountains, often walking at night. In daylight, columns of refugees leaving Ethiopia were strafed by government airplanes.

In early November 1984, the first refugees from Tigre crossed the border into Sudan and stopped near a rock formation called Tukulubab, near the city of Kassala. This first famine camp in Sudan became labeled "the death camp" by the world press. Forty thousand people arrived at Tukulubab over the next month.

They were forced to congregate at a desolate spot. Food and water had to be carried in by truck. By January 1985 fuel was so scarce that it was impossible to run trucks with enough water for the camp. The daily water ration of two to three liters per person was inadequate for cooking and drinking in a windy climate with more than one-hundred-degree heat. (Refugee experts recommend at least 15 liters per person daily; an average American uses 120.) On certain days near the end, no water at all was delivered.

Evacuation of Tukulubab began in December 1984. Refugees were moved by truck 350 kilometers to the interior, to reception sites that were being set up hastily near the Sudanese village of El Fau. These new camps—Fau 1, 2, and 3—were located along the Rahad Canal, a muddy, polluted, 100-foot-wide irrigation ditch coming off the Blue Nile.

The migration continued. As December 1984 began, refugees were entering Sudan farther south, near the village of Wad Kowli. This camp on the Atbara River now became the doorway out of Tigre, and by the end of January 1985, Wad Kowli had swelled to more than ninety thousand people. Within a few months the river ran dry, and in March 1985 evacuation of Wad Kowli began.

(opposite)
Map of Eastern Sudan.

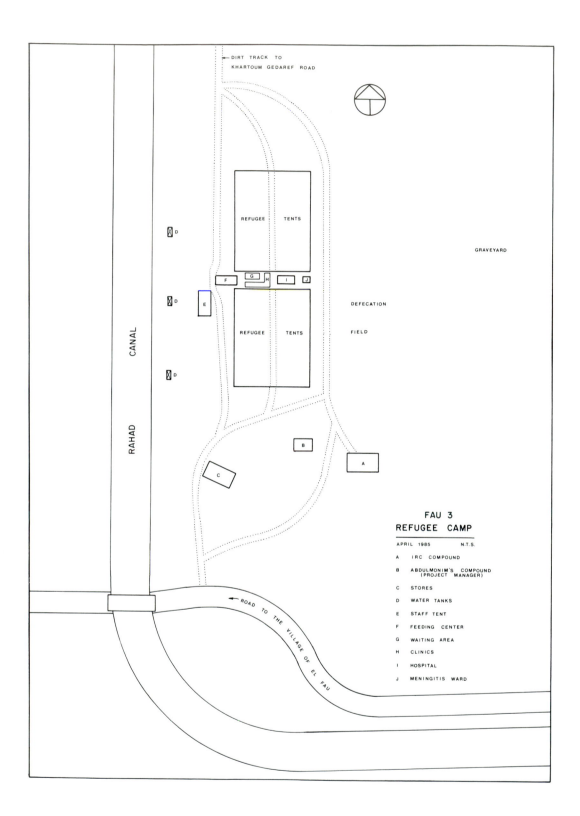

← DIRT TRACK TO
KHARTOUM GEDAREF ROAD

REFUGEE TENTS

GRAVEYARD

X D

F   G   H   I   J

X D   E

DEFECATION

REFUGEE TENTS   FIELD

X D

CANAL

RAHAD

B

A

C

FAU 3
REFUGEE CAMP

APRIL 1985   N.T.S.

A   IRC COMPOUND

B   ABDULMONIM'S COMPOUND
        (PROJECT MANAGER)

C   STORES

D   WATER TANKS

E   STAFF TENT

F   FEEDING CENTER

G   WAITING AREA

H   CLINICS

I   HOSPITAL

J   MENINGITIS WARD

← ROAD TO THE VILLAGE OF EL FAU

Tukulubab to Fau 3

In January 1985, while the redirected flood of refugees reached Wad Kowli, the brief drama of Tukulubab played its final scene. By this time there were five graveyards, and at the newest site one could count more than two hundred graves. Most of the graves were just heaps of sand without identification, and many were extremely small. Vultures circled overhead.

As food, water, and supplies ran out, the pressure to empty Tukulubab increased. Between January 24 and February 8, 1985, the last thirteen thousand people were evacuated to Fau 3. It became a desperate race with disaster. Families were split up. The hospitals, the sick, the dislocated who had been held back were now shipped all at once. Fifty to seventy people were crowded into each closed truck for the seven-hour trip. There was no food or water during the trip.

In every few trucks that arrived at Fau 3, workers for IRC (International Rescue Committee, the New York–based relief group with whom I had enlisted) found a corpse. There is no record of how many died in transit. A small handful of IRC and Sudanese workers frantically tried to prepare the barren site. They did not know how many refugees were coming each night or when they would arrive. One night fifty-four trucks holding thirty-six hundred people arrived between 3:00 and 6:30 A.M., and one truck actually drove into the Rahad Canal. Twins were born in that truck. Miraculously, both survived.

In those first few days at Fau 3, the misery was overwhelming. Tents were not up yet, and the refugees begged for anything to use as shelter against the relentless sun. People even pressed their bodies against the few leafless thorn bushes trying to find shade, and some remained without shelter the entire first week.

Joan Porter was the first doctor in Fau 3. She helped unload the trucks. The hospital was a thatch shelter, and Joan

(opposite)
Map of Fau 3
refugee camp.

slept in the hospital on a mat because living quarters for the expatriates were not yet built. In a single day she recorded thirty-two hospital deaths. Many of the people died before she had a chance to examine them.

A prepackaged "disaster medical kit" was provided. It was designed to last three months in a disaster involving ten thousand people; it was gone in less than three weeks. Then Donna Mosely, the second doctor to arrive, scrounged from the local markets ingredients for homemade oral rehydration fluids for malnourished infants suffering from diarrhea. She complained bitterly that it had been impossible to find the necessary potassium to put in the solution, and she watched several infants die as a result. Later, a nurse arrived from Khartoum and brought generous stocks of packaged oral rehydration salts from the United Nations International Children's Emergency Fund (UNICEF) that had been sitting in the UNICEF Khartoum warehouse all along. This was typical of the crippling lack of communication that affected everything. Eastern Sudan is a region without telephones. The only way to communicate is by short-wave radio, but radios were prohibited by the Sudanese.

All supplies were hard to obtain, and nothing was easy or could be taken for granted. The sanitarian had to spend most of his time looking for black-market fuel for the water pumps, or else the refugees would be without water. At first the medicines at Fau 1 and 2 were stored outside in the sun, and when Donna organized the pharmacy at Fau 3, every shelf was a minor triumph. The entire camp, a makeshift city for thirteen thousand, had been scraped together in three weeks. Chairs, tables, beds, water barrels, paper, pens, cooking pots—everything—had to be found and put into place. Fuel remained in short supply, and in the beginning there was no vehicle for the new camp. A vehicle came to Fau 3 every two or three days. Otherwise the camp was isolated. The expatriates could not communicate with the outside or leave.

Conflicts within the Camps

Local staff for the IRC health and sanitation programs had to be assembled, a task as difficult as securing supplies, because of typical African tribal conflicts. IRC brought in staff who worked with IRC elsewhere, and this staff was Amharic, mostly English-speaking young men from Addis Ababa who had been in Sudan for several years. They were political refugees. Many had been students and had come to Sudan to avoid military service with the Dergue. Some had been tortured. They hoped for a future in Canada or the United States. They were different from the famine refugees, peasant farmers who intended to return to their highland farms. Tigrayans have generations of mistrust and hatred for the Amharics. They speak different languages.

Antagonisms were further complicated by political problems between IRC and REST. Although the refugees from Tigre were organized and led out of Ethiopia by REST, in Sudan REST was not officially recognized or given power. As the refugees were divided in different camps, the skeleton group of REST leadership sent to Sudan was scattered and undercut. In this sensitive setting, political blunders were made. An uninformed IRC doctor, in an interview for Reuters wire service just after the Fau camps opened, stated that many of the refugees were brought out of Tigre at gunpoint by REST. This fantastic and untrue public statement infuriated REST, an organization dependent on international aid.

Angry conflicts disrupted the medical clinics. REST made accusations: the Amharic workers were not working hard; they were uncaring for the refugees; they were an enemy tribe, Dergue spies. Accusations about REST were made in return. There were confrontations about who should be hired and fired. Threats were reported by numerous Amharic workers. Almost no one in REST spoke English, which complicated getting stories straight and settling disputes.

Crisis Point

Disaster warnings had been ignored. No one was prepared. But in the face of innumerable obstacles, IRC, with a tiny refugee health program established several years before, attempted to extend care to 120,000 additional refugees. By March 1985 IRC had brought forty-one expatriate doctors, nurses, and sanitarians to the camps.

The IRC administrators were as overwhelmed as the medical staff. In February 1985 the program director, Tim White, dispatched a handwritten note to New York headquarters. Everything was in crisis, the other administrator was too sick to work, and he was working as long as he could stretch the day to keep supplies and people moving to the medical staff in the camps. Then Tim contracted both amoebic dysentery and malaria, and he was forced to bed for two weeks.

It was in the midst of this confusion and misery that I arrived in Sudan. Perhaps nothing could have prepared me for what I found.

SNAKES, SCORPIONS, AND THE FIRST PLAGUE

Fau 3 Refugee Camp, March 2–March 25, 1985

(opposite)
Fau 3 refugee camp, March 1985. Coptic priest.

March 2, 1985

As we drove closer to Fau 3, the landscape became increasingly barren. There was a single tree in the compound at Fau 1 and no trees at Fau 2. I felt that we had left Africa and were driving through endless desolation. We followed a dirt track that ran parallel to the Rahad Canal. We couldn't see the canal, only the twenty-foot mound of excavated dirt that ran alongside. On the other side of our car was empty, baked, black cracked dirt that stretched to the horizon.

I can't believe it's only four days since I left New York City. It seems like another lifetime since I met Amy Greer, who is to be my coworker, at the International Departures lounge at JFK Airport. Her huge pile of luggage, with a large stuffed animal perched on top, made me wonder what she expected. She told me about her nursing background in intensive care and cardiac surgery. We talked about work outside the United States. She seemed confident because of experience in Saudi Arabia and in volunteering with a group of plastic surgeons that make weekend trips to Central America. I wonder if the bleak warnings we get every day have affected her expectations like they have mine.

Khartoum Airport felt like Times Square packed into a shed. Khartoum itself was a disappointment compared to the intriguing image brought to mind by the city's name. The city was hot, flat, and dusty, with many unpaved streets. Most of the buildings were low, shabby concrete-block structures. The Nile was low and muddy brown.

In Khartoum the UNICEF representative to the Sudan told me that 4.5 million Sudanese would be starving like the Ethiopians if the May rains again failed. Our talk was cut short by an emergency telex requesting that he provide information for a debate on the famine that was in progress in London, in the British House of Commons.

The short time in Khartoum is already blurred in my mind,

but the five-hour drive from Khartoum to Gedaref was too ominous to forget.

To pass the time I counted dead animals lying by the side of the road. In less than fifteen minutes, I'd counted twenty camels and cows desiccating in the heat. They were not road kills. The animals were abandoned, because the nomads haven't enough water.

The night we arrived in Gedaref from Khartoum, I sat up late talking with two of the IRC administrators. It was dark except for a kerosene lantern flickering on the table between us. They both seemed painfully exhausted but past the point of bothering, like people so tired that sleep will no longer come. When we sat down it had just gotten dark. Lights were on, but after a few minutes the electricity went off. The fan overhead gradually slowed down and stopped. We sat in the dark for several minutes before anyone got up to find a lantern. The town (and country) is short of fuel, so electricity is erratic. I learned that the program director for IRC is sick and that he has been unable to get out of bed for the last two weeks.

I also learned that Amy Greer and I—the two new recruits—were headed for Fau 3, the refugee camp described as the "pressure cooker" by the administrator of the group of camps (Fau 1, 2, and 3) near the Sudanese village of El Fau. Fau 3 was the last camp formed in the disastrous evacuation of Tukulubab. Only about a month old, it has the sickest population, the worst political problems, and the least organized expatriate staff.

In New York and again in Khartoum, I had been told that I would go to Wad Kowli, on the Ethiopian border, to work with my friend Martha who has been at Wad Kowli for almost a month. I had looked forward to working with Martha. She and I had worked together in a refugee camp in Somalia and during emergency immunization in Uganda.

When the administrator made his announcement about Fau 3, I initially resisted. There were already five medical people, including two doctors, at Fau 3. The public health nurse, Sarah Barr, had worked in Somalia and is doing fine; but I was told that the two doctors, Joan and Donna, who have no prior refugee camp experience, are not getting along with each other. Worst off are Tom and Candy McDonald, a husband-wife team of nurse practitioners that arrived three weeks ago. Tom has been sick almost the entire time, and the administrator plans to pick the couple up for a week's vacation in Khartoum when we are dropped off. He thinks they should be sent home. Still, on paper it looks like all the camps are staffed equally thin. I don't want to go somewhere primarily to solve a personality conflict—particularly not one between two doctors. IRC has no doctor at Wad Kowli.

We sat around in Gedaref for two more days waiting for the medical director. I visited the program director, Tim White, in his bedroom. He's still too weak to get up, almost too weak to talk. I couldn't sleep. I had jet lag, with days and nights mixed up, and it's too hot to sleep in the day. I left New York with the flu, and now I've caught bronchitis. With all the dust I cough constantly, and at night I'm embarrassed that I might be keeping this crowded house awake.

The medical director was due any time, but no one could say exactly when. He has to hitchhike, and the only vehicles on the roads are called Suk lorries, old English Bedford trucks that appear to be left over from World War II. There is a severe shortage of vehicles. There are no phones, and relief agencies are not allowed to have short-wave radios.

The medical director finally arrived late last night, dusty, with a three-day beard, a bandanna around his neck and Walkman headphones. He had just come in from the Fau camps, and he looked like someone that had been camping out for a month. No question the medical need is greatest at Fau 3, with uncontrollable numbers of sick people in the clinics and a terrible shortage of supplies. Also, besides difficulties with the IRC expatriates, there are major problems with the large

Ethiopian staff. I was relieved to know from another doctor why I was going to Fau 3, although it sounds horrific. If I can get the situation under control in a month, I still would like to go to Wad Kowli. I told him this.

This morning Amy and I were asked to be ready to leave at 7:00 A.M. Then we sat, like baggage placed by the door. There was no breakfast. At 2:00 P.M. Amy and I started searching the house for food. There was an atmosphere of such rush and crisis that to ask about food seemed petty. We left the IRC house in Gedaref just after 4:00 P.M.

If there had been an acceptable way to get back in the land rover and drive away from Fau 3 refugee camp, I might have done so the moment we arrived. Nobody even got up to greet us. It felt like we had come, uninvited, into a very private and personal grief. Five people—Joan, Donna, Sarah, Tom, and Candy—sat in the IRC compound. They looked on the verge of tears.

I thought back to the night I'd arrived on the Thai-Cambodian border in 1980. There had been a welcome party, followed by enthusiastic orientation. In Somalia, Martha, the team leader, had given new staff a tour explaining day-to-day life in the compound. In Uganda the bishop had hosted a welcome dinner for our emergency immunization team.

Then I looked at the scene in this desolate place called Fau 3. Joan was making corn fritters over an open charcoal fire —one small corn fritter for each person. Opening the single tin of canned corn had evidently been an event. There were only five cans in the cupboard, and they were being hoarded. Comments such as "Oh Joan, this is such a good dinner," "Isn't this wonderful," and "What a treat" were offered as if none of this was really happening, as if this was a slow-motion, melancholy dream.

After dinner the guard, Siam, announced that two people were there to see Sarah. Without explanation she got up and walked off with them in the black night. I learned that they

(page 28)
Fau 3 refugee camp, March 1985. On my first morning in camp, I walked a quarter of a mile past rows of dusty brown tents to the clinic.

were two of the translators, Amharics, and that they had been "threatened" by REST. Sarah returned forty-five minutes later. Several of the workers were going to quit. Then it was Joan's turn to walk off into the night, also into camp, more than a kilometer away, to see if she could "talk things out."

I brought out chocolate from our stopover in Zurich. It was now a liquid mess from the heat. After eating their portion and hardly saying a word, Tom and Candy went off to bed. The rest of us sat up and talked. I wanted to know about the camp. It was obvious that a political crisis was going on. I was filled with uncertainty, but tonight nothing was explained. Sarah, Donna, and Joan brushed my questions aside, and I was depressed and shaken to realize that from my first minute in camp I was being excluded.

I ended the day lying in bed with the most disturbing feelings since I left New York. I have joined an exhausted group under ferocious emotional stress, and they seem reluctant to include newcomers who are outside their circle of pain.

March 3

The first thing I noticed this morning is that there are no birds at Fau 3. Birds, acacia thorn trees, vast horizons, harsh sun—these are the African bush. On this continent birds are the spirit of life. In Somalia a family of large doves with strange red eye feathers had nested in a thorn tree hanging over my tent. I had to duck under the branches to get into my tent, and when I left my tent I often stared eye to eye with the doves from four feet away; every morning their cooing had awakened me just before dawn. A ragtag group of noisy, colored birds had been my alarm clock in Uganda where we slept in the servant quarters of an old British colonial estate. They perched on the window and in the tree beside the window just before first light. Twice in Uganda we worked under trees with weaver birds, those brilliant golden yellow birds that hang

(opposite)
Fau 3 refugee camp, March 1985. Hospital patient with malnutrition and pneumonia.

their strange oval nests upside down, hundreds in a single tree. We'd pause from immunizing and look up at a tree full of birds fussing with their nests.

Here the silent sunrise feels like a violation of nature. It leaves an empty space, like the quiet at a funeral, a silence that signifies a break in the normal flow of life. It is another powerful sign of things gone wrong.

March 4

It's not clear where Amy Greer and I are supposed to fit in or what we should do. I sense unspoken issues of turf despite so much needing to be done. We still haven't talked, and yesterday was not a glorious beginning.

I woke up still sick. By 8:00 A.M. the sun was so hot it felt like my skin would turn brittle and crack like the baked clay dirt. I was thirsty as soon as I woke up. The water filter was clogged with mud. There was no filtered water left, and there was no breakfast.

We walked about a quarter of a mile past rows of dusty brown tents to the clinic. There I saw a crowd of people surrounding the thatch building waiting to be seen. They all looked resigned and exhausted. Inside people sat on straw mats on the ground. Dust was everywhere. Some people, too ill to sit up, lay covered with blankets despite the heat. One skeletally thin 5-year-old girl was racked with spasms of coughing until tears ran down her cheeks. As I watched, her father rubbed her back and tried to soothe her. I realized after one look that she was dying of malnutrition and TB. I learned that there are no medicines to treat TB.

I watched Donna see child after child in the clinic. It was to be a day of tagging along to see how things are done. There was only one translator, so it was impossible to see patients myself. One of the first children needed to be hospitalized. After the translator explained, the mother began crying. It was an unwanted surprise. In Somalia the refugees had been fatalistic Muslims. No matter what happened, they never cried. If anyone had lost control, it had been us. This tearful outburst shattered a barrier that I had unconsciously remembered. It brought me uncomfortably close.

Then Donna examined a 10-year-old boy whom she and Joan had treated without success. The child had a swelling on the shaft of his penis. There appeared to be a small tract draining pus. I thought it was an abscess that needed to be opened and drained, and after giving an anesthetic injection I made a small incision. No pus came out. It was my first patient, and all I had done was make things worse. I dressed the wound and got some new medicine, which I gave to the father. I told him to bring his son back, and I would try another medicine if this failed. With solemn formality the father and his boy both shook my hand. Their gratitude gave me a hollow, sick feeling after the mistake I had just made.

Things went no better in the seventy-bed hospital, where many of the patients will obviously die. For a while I followed Joan in her distraught pilgrimage from one bed to the next. Then I found someone who spoke enough English for me to work independently. The beds are arranged in five long rows. I started at the other end of the ward, at the first bed of row E. At the last bed in row E, I cried.

A 25-year-old woman and her 2-year-old daughter shared the bed. The mother has been treated with all our available antibiotics. She is feverish and weak. Nothing has helped. She has been coughing up blood for the past four months and is obviously dying of tuberculosis. She is too weak to take care of her child, and the child is fed by the sick woman in the next bed. The child is malnourished and covered with flies. We have no drugs to treat the woman's tuberculosis, and her cough is highly infectious. To protect the other patients, we should send her out. There is nothing more we can do for her, and we need the bed for other sick people. But the translator

(page 34)
Fau 3 refugee camp,
March 23, 1985. Joan
Porter has had a fever on
and off for a week, and
today we noticed that her
eyes are yellow. She has
hepatitis and will go home.

tells me she does not have a tent and that she has been separated from her husband and village. The translator says they are at Wad Kowli, but it is impossible to communicate or travel between here and there. If she is sent out, no one will care for her child, and the child will die.

I stood there overwhelmed with responsibility to do something. Any action I could take seemed monstrously inhumane. To do nothing seemed like avoiding my job and seemed equally unfair.

(I did nothing but told myself I would speak to Joan. Other problems rapidly pushed this woman out of my mind. Several days later I went to find her. She had died. I searched but never found the child.)

Amy's first day went no better. Tom and Candy, for at least the coming week, are gone. The nutritionist who runs the Therapeutic Feeding Center, also left for a few days, so the feeding center was Amy's logical place.

Amy Greer was faced with several hundred crying, coughing, fly-covered, starving kids packed in a hot thatch structure. The children sit on mats on the ground with a parent or older sibling, and the bodies are so crowded that it's difficult to walk across the enclosure without stepping on a baby. Many have diarrhea, and there is no place to take them. The place smells. The temperature outside is 110 degrees. Inside this cramped shelter with so many bodies and no breeze, it feels smothering and overwhelming. The sounds of feeble crying and coughing come from every direction.

Malnutrition is diagnosed by measuring the child's height and weight. If a child weighs less than 85 percent of the predicted weight for a measured height, that child is, technically, malnourished. Here children are not counted in that category unless they are under 80 percent, and by that criteria between one-third and one-half of the children in this camp are malnourished. If they are under 70 percent, they are "severely malnourished" and are sent all day to the Therapeutic Feed-

(opposite)
Fau 3 refugee camp, March 1985. A child recovering from measles.

ing Center, which serves six high-calorie meals over the course of the day.

Most of the children Amy found in the feeding center were under 5 years old. Children that age are the most vulnerable to malnutrition. If the mother is alive, a child is usually well fed until leaving the mother's breast, at about six months of age. Then follows the period of greatest jeopardy. The child is growing most rapidly, has the greatest nutritional and metabolic needs, but is not yet able to feed itself. The child will compete unsuccessfully with other hungry mouths. And the child has not yet had the common illnesses such as measles or whooping cough, which exacerbate malnutrition. Finally, it's a cruel fact that little children are the most expendable. Older children can work, and if the parents starve they know that all of their children risk death.

It takes no measuring to appreciate this situation. I've seen children 10 or 13 years old with severe malnutrition, an indication of extremely bad conditions. I've also seen frightening cases. Fifty-five children in this camp are less than 60 percent of their predicted weight. They are pitiful skeletons, sometimes too weak to cry, and it is impossible for me to look at them and not remember pictures of Dachau or Buchenwald.

I left Amy Greer in the feeding center at 8:00 A.M. She had a tough time figuring out how to begin. When I went back at the end of the day, the place looked like a Fellini circus. Most of these skeletal children had mouths painted purple, or irregular blotches of purple on their shaved heads. They looked like pathetic clowns.

Amy had started by treating every child that had scalp ringworm, or thrush (yeast infection of the mouth), with Gentian Violet. She did something graphically visible to defy feeling overwhelmed.

March 5

Our guard, Siam, and our cook, Eiosis, refugees in their late
40s, carry themselves with a sad paternal air. Neither speaks
a word of English, but they both speak a little Italian, a relic
of Ethiopia's colonial past. Siam will occasionally try a few
words in Italian out of frustration when we don't understand
something. They are not subservient, and our relationship is
different from any at home. It is almost as if Siam regards
us as children whose care has been entrusted to him, children who think they are capable of looking after themselves
but really aren't. He is responsible for seeing that we come to
no harm, and he takes a great interest in us. Eiosis is gentle,
speaks quietly, and covers her mouth in shyness whenever she
smiles. She arrives in the morning with a black shawl wrapped
around her head that she carefully takes off and folds. She also
takes off her shoes, and she puts them away with the shawl.
In the evening before she leaves she puts her shoes and shawl
back on.

Today was food distribution day in camp, distributed to
each head of family. Each person got a ration that is expected
to last fifteen days:

> 3 packages spaghetti
> 900 grams lentils
> 3 kilograms flour
> 150 grams salt
> 150 grams chile peppers
> oil (a few cups)
> charcoal for cooking fires

Sarah Barr tells me that up to now each ration has been
different depending, she thinks, on which country was donor.
What is the same, she says, is that before the end of each
period most people are without food.

Sarah is in charge of public health. Her work takes her
inside the tents, where the rest of us rarely go. Sarah is doing

exactly what needs to be done. She is training a group of thirty in primary health care: recognition and treatment of simple common problems, particularly diarrhea and dehydration. Her workers go tent to tent distributing soap and razors when these items are available. They record births and deaths. They try to find sick people. Only about half of the malnourished children show up at the Therapeutic Feeding Center, and Sarah's group tries to find the children who fail to come. They distribute shrouds. They report to Sarah when tents are blown over or ripped by the wind, and Sarah gives the list of destroyed tents to Abdulmonim, the project manager (Sudanese camp director), who sends help to repitch them.

They also report to Sarah things that she can do nothing about—like the fifty-four old people. Sarah carries this list around with her and brings it out for discussion at every camp meeting: "What are we going to do about the fifty-four old people who are sick and separated from their families and villages and lying in tents unable to care for themselves?" They are victims of the social disruption of the move from Tigre and then from Tukulubab. REST has said they will make an old-age home, and Sarah takes out this list of neglected people, whom she says will die before anything gets done.

Today we were visited by a medical school dean from the board of directors of IRC. He's here to evaluate programs in Sudan, and he obviously cares about us and about helping the refugees. He worked on the Thai-Cambodian border and apparently sees things based on that experience. In Thailand resources were plentiful, and most of our efforts were spent on curative medical care. Lessons from Thailand are a curse here, and his last question gave it all away. "Have you coded anyone yet?" he asked, meaning had we tried cardiac resuscitation on someone who died. "Coding" someone is a symbol of curative medicine at any cost. It is as medically appropriate to this camp as diet pills. Joan said that she had.

I gave our visitor a small package to drop off at UNICEF

in Khartoum for the diplomatic pouch to New York. I have photographed for UNICEF in Somalia and Uganda. It was the first six rolls of film of the camp—my first impressions—plus a letter to the UNICEF photo chief, Jim Breetveld, written by flashlight at 11:00 P.M. last night, when I was exhausted and overwhelmed by my first days in this place. This horror must be seen, I thought over and over to myself as I fought sleep and wrote Breetveld. When I handed him the film, I explained that UNICEF was waiting for information and would make good use of fresh news from Sudan. If I get only one good picture, please let it be now when it might do some good.

(The film and letter were lost, which I learned three months later when I got back to New York.)

March 6

The hospital is not working, despite the best intentions. We are spending too much time trying to cure people near death, at the expense of preventing illness. Right now we face epidemic malnutrition, polluted water, no immunization, inadequate shelter, no sanitation, and a disrupted social fabric. If we cure someone's illness in the hospital, he will only get sick again because we send him out to starve, freeze at night, and drink polluted water. If basic human necessities were provided, we probably wouldn't need a hospital. Hospitals are an overwhelming political symbol of help, but I see them as a trap for our good intentions and a symbol that leaders and policymakers don't understand the priorities.

Too many Western doctors fight the wrong battles. Like Joan, who leaves for the hospital about six each morning and returns after dark every night, usually close to 9:00 P.M. She spends her entire day in the hospital making rounds, examining and reexamining patients, many of whom are certain to die. She starts intravenous lines, but under current circumstances these seem largely impractical. We have few or no

(page 42)
Fau 3 refugee camp, March 1985. Banks of the Rahad Canal on the west edge of camp.

satisfactory needles, and we are often out of tape. In the ten or fifteen minutes while an intravenous line is being started, every worker in the ward stops work and crowds around to watch. Attention is diverted from more important but unexciting tasks, like feeding and giving oral rehydration. These hard and messy tasks are often neglected. Meanwhile, most of the intravenous lines do not last an hour. In a furious doctor's scrawl on tattered scraps of paper, Joan writes daily notes on each patient: "medical records" that no one will ever read. In most cases we will never prove or disprove the diagnosis, because we lack the necessary tests, and much of the illness we will never treat because we lack the means.

We spent at least an hour yesterday morning looking for tape and tearing up index cards to mark the beds of several new patients. We made squares for patients needing half-strength milk and circles for patients needing full-strength milk. But at the same time, the entire hospital receives inadequate food.

Still worse, almost three-quarters of the deaths so far have occurred outside the hospital, unreached and largely ignored by our system of health care. How many of those deaths out in the camp were children with malnutrition and simple diarrhea, children who could have been saved? Hospital medicine is not the answer if we hope to solve the health problems of this camp. It doesn't matter that we're doing things for admirable reasons, and it doesn't matter how hard we try. It's like throwing a tennis ball straight up in the air with all your strength, trying to hit the moon.

(opposite)
Fau 3 refugee camp, March 1985. The pharmacy.

(page 46)
Fau 3 refugee camp, March 13, 1985. Halima in the Therapeutic Feeding Center, refusing food offered by her sister.

March 7

The outpatient clinic is a long thatch hut divided into five areas. It faces a large, thatched sun shelter called a *recuba*, where people wait. About 250 to 300 people come to the clinic each day. Ten or twenty people sleep under the *recuba* overnight, hoping for a favorable place in line for the next day.

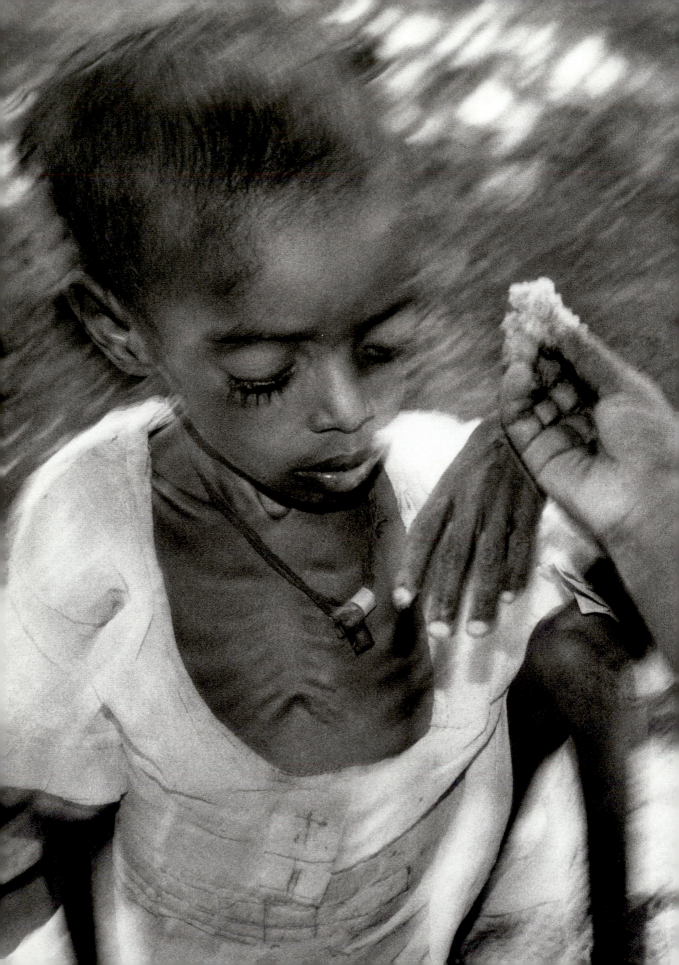

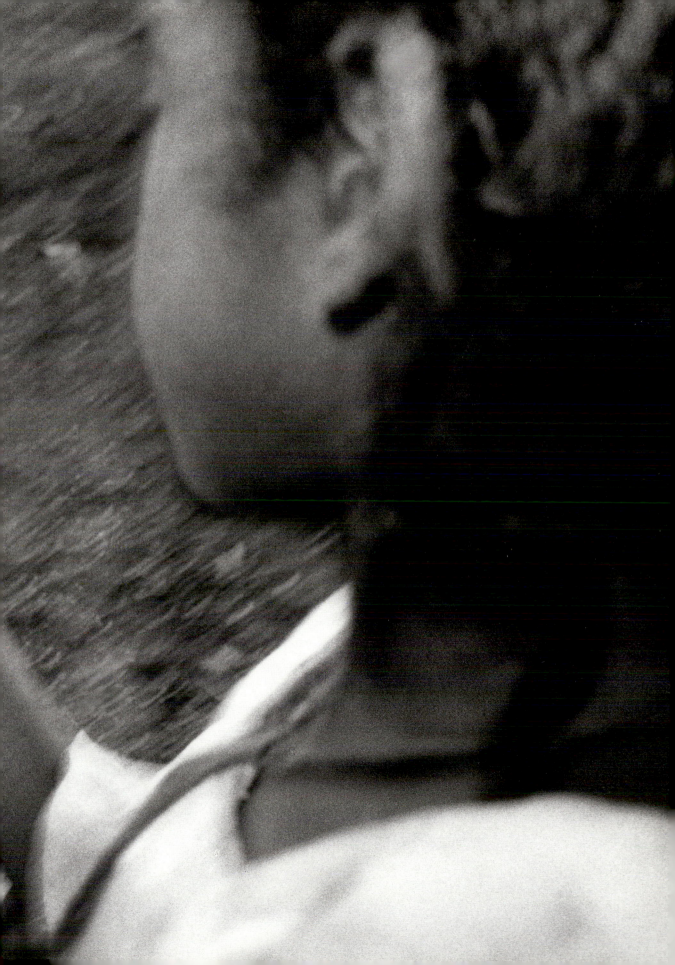

The first area is registration and screening. Several refugees (with no medical background except for Sarah's cram course) prescribe treatment for most complaints by simple formula. They have not been taught how to examine a patient or inquire about symptoms in any depth. A person who complains of fever and chills is prescribed treatment for malaria, chloroquine for three days. A person with cough and fever gets an antibiotic for pneumonia. Cough without fever is a cold; no antibiotics. The list of diseases and treatments is short but elastic. People who can walk and don't look too sick receive superficial attention and are sent away.

Sicker patients go to the next room and see one of the two trained Ethiopian examiners, Donna, or me. The third area is for oral rehydration, a separate room where we send all patients with dehydration and diarrhea. Diarrhea is a leading cause of death, and if dehydration is prevented with the proper amounts of fluids mixed with sugar and salts, most of the deaths can be prevented. Then comes the treatment room (for injections), the pharmacy, and two rooms for teaching and public health.

The clinic goes slowly, because we are short of translators. There are only five people in the entire camp who are fluent in both Tigrinyan and English. One of them translates for Joan in the hospital, and the other four have important jobs and can not be spared just to translate. So far I've tried using a translator for whom I actually have to pantomime. I've sometimes used two translators—the first translates from English into Amharic, and the second translates from Amharic into Tigrinyan. Then the answer from the patient has to come back by the same route. The answers often make no sense. The translators pretend to understand the questions and answers, because they fear exposing how little of the language they actually know. The translator jobs are prized. It's painful to see how hard they try while lacking the essential skill, and it's frustrating to constantly wait for information that usually doesn't help.

The most common disease in the clinic has been dysentery, bloody diarrhea, because we ran out of chlorine for the water supply. Somebody sent us alum by mistake, which we used for about two weeks. Each day the sanitation assistant tested the chlorine level in the drinking water and announced that the water was "OK."

Alum is used to precipitate the gross impurities in the water and cause it to settle to the bottom of the tank. Alum is helpful if the water is filtered or drawn off the top of the tank. The tanks we have draw from the bottom, from where all the polluted sludge ends up.

This foul water has given between one-quarter and one-third of the camp bloody diarrhea, and it has probably killed some of the malnourished children. The pharmacy shelves are rapidly emptying of Septra, tetracycline, ampicillin, and chloramphenicol—antibiotics to treat diarrhea. All this medicine has little effect, because the refugees continue drinking the polluted unchlorinated water. They can't boil it, because we are short of fuel. There is no wood on the site. Some of them get up at 3:00 or 4:00 A.M. to walk several hours looking for wood, but they use it to improve their living compound, making windbreaks and better shelter. Besides, no one wants to make extra fires. It's 110 degrees outside.

What this camp obviously needs more than antibiotics, hospitals, or doctors are a few cheap drums of chlorine.

March 8

I went in to the clinic at 7:00 A.M., and about an hour later someone ran in shouting Amy's name and motioning me to follow. In the feeding center I found Amy standing over a 4-year-old girl in a coma taking what looked like her last breaths. The child was skeletal. The final event in these cases will sometimes be dehydration and a sharp decline in the blood sugar. We took a bottle of intravenous fluid containing dextrose, and I showed Amy where to insert the needle directly into the child's abdomen. Fluid ran in for two or three minutes, and to our amazement the child revived. Her eyes opened, and, very feebly at first, she began to move her arms and then to cry.

I wrote a note for Joan telling what happened. We had not noticed the mother at first. We found her waiting in silence only a few feet away, sitting on the ground with her face covered. Amy and I felt an excited euphoria. We had saved a life. But in spite of our success, the mother's eyes showed only pain and loss, and her face still glistened with tears. We found a translator and explained for her to carry her daughter to the hospital with the note for Joan. (In the hospital the child lived one more day.)

I returned to the clinic and saw patients until 2:00 P.M. I tried working without a translator. Using a list of about fifty Tigrinyan words prepared with several of the workers late yesterday afternoon over a few cups of tea, my questions were limited to fever, cough, and diarrhea.

I saw many patients with unusual illnesses often caused by lack of vitamins. Many people have unexplained swelling (edema) of their legs or abdomen, or of the scrotum in men. This is probably a form of wet beriberi, caused by thiamine deficiency. Another form of thiamine deficiency, called dry beriberi, affects the nerves. There are many people who complain of burning or pain in their hand or feet, and some people have trouble with balance, walk with a very wide gait or can't walk at all. Thiamine deficiency can also cause altered behavior, even psychosis. There are people in camp like that too, but it's impossible to be certain of the cause. Our vitamin tablets don't have adequate thiamine to treat these patients.

Pellagra, caused by niacin deficiency, is in this camp as well. The word comes from Italian, meaning "rough skin." We find patches of what looks like crocodile skin on the forearm or shin, in areas exposed to the sun. I had seen one case on the Cambodian border in 1980. Here the disease is common. Lack of niacin also causes diarrhea and dementia, but in Fau 3 there are so many other reasons for those problems that it's impossible to tell what the cause is for every symptom.

We wrack our brains trying to sort out these bizarre vitamin problems, and we search through the medical books to figure out the correct treatment. Then we rummage through the pharmacy trying to find the right medicines. Often the tablets are the wrong dose, or we need injection and only have pills, or our supply is already exhausted. We send urgent messages for more medicines. What a costly, dismal substitute for decent food.

I walked back to our compound in the middle of the afternoon, dehydrated, exhausted, spirits numb. I drank a full liter of water, had a bucket shower, and then drank more water. I put on a wet shirt and wet shorts, and sat in my *tukul* hoping to cool off. The water evaporating from my clothing made me feel cool and comfortable for only fifteen minutes. Then my shirt and shorts were bone dry.

Everyone who was back in the compound gradually wandered into my *tukul*. There are now three hammocks strung up, and with my cot it's a place we can gather. In Somalia we worked out camp problems while lying around in the hammocks at night. Perhaps setting this up will help us organize ourselves better as a team. We talked about improving the way we feed the hospital patients. Several people alluded to the lack of understanding or agreement about our priorities and who is responsible for what tasks.

March 9

Amy Greer was evacuated from camp today, after lying in her *tukul* off and on for several days. She is being taken back to Gedaref. She worked less than a week before getting sick. I think she caught amoebic dysentery from our water.

Her illness makes me think about the difficulty I'm having

trying to get settled. I've gradually realized that there is no daily routine. There's no administrator or logistics person in this camp, and none of the doctors or nurses has taken the time or had the energy to organize how we expatriates live, eat, or will maintain our health. It goes deeper than that, as if taking decent care of ourselves would be some form of violation in the face of so much misery that we are failing to relieve.

The *tukuls*, the round straw huts we live in, are dusty beyond belief. Insects crawl through the straw walls and drop from the ceiling. At night the wind blows through, and during the day the *tukuls* give no insulation from the heat. Even the poorest Sudanese mud up the walls of their *tukuls*. There is no field shower. To wash we stand on a handful of straw in the mud and pour a bucketful of water over ourselves, cup by cup. Eiosis cooks dinner, but no one tells her what to make. There is no organized breakfast, not even a fire started and water boiled. Eiosis would come in early and help, but Joan says "I can't bear to have those people around so early in the morning. I just want peace and quiet." There is an emotional tone implying that eating breakfast is an indulgence. Joan does not stop or come back to the compound for lunch, and no lunch is prepared. No one has taken the effort to arrange it, work out a menu, or find a translator to arrange things with Eiosis.

Joan, Donna, Sarah, Tom, and Candy have been working themselves to exhaustion the last few weeks. Everyone but Candy has been sick. Joan was here first and set a standard of physical exertion, suffering, and self-denial that no one can maintain for long. The rest of the group, punchy with fatigue and emotionally overwhelmed, stagger on this path behind her. Our living circumstances and medical priorities seem intertwined.

At breakfast today I again asked that Joan, Donna, and I have a talk. I said we needed to work on priorities and organization of the team. Joan said she was too busy for meetings and too tired at the end of the day, and then looked away. I finally

(opposite)
Fau 3 refugee camp, March 1985. Malnourished child in the hospital.

insisted, and the meeting was set for 6:00 A.M. tomorrow. Joan walked off to camp. Donna followed me into my *tukul* and asked me not to interfere with Joan's work, to let her continue doing what she wants. (The meeting never happened.)

March 10

Journalists and politicians steadily come through camp, because we are near the only paved road going east, toward the Ethiopian border and other camps. Most of the visitors are glassy-eyed from jet lag and heat, and they are horrified that babies are indeed starving. Today there was someone different, a reporter from the *Los Angeles Times*, familiar with the scene and unsurprised at the starvation and misery. In the form of questions, he proposed a cold-blooded and cynical view: Who ever heard of Tigre before these starving people arrived in Sudan? Now their story, pictures of their starving babies, and calls for support are front-page news around the world. What would have happened to the TPLF in the civil war if all the peasants went to government relief centers instead of Sudan? Underneath it all, what mixture of hopes and motives really set this dramatic catastrophe in motion?

March 11

4:00 A.M.

It took me just over a week to get sick. I have cramps and diarrhea. Since midnight it's been impossible to sleep. One month here will be my physical limit, and I will be lucky if I last that long.

AFTERNOON

In between visits to the latrine, I've been trying to remember what we did in Somalia four years ago. I've brought the kitchen table into my *tukul* to use as a desk. I sit here, with a

pencil in one hand and Pepto-Bismol in the other. I'm draft-
ing a set of simple descriptions of the most common medical
problems with simple instructions on how to treat.

In this chaos, overwhelming needs send us in every direction. With no guidelines we get lost. On a deeper level, there
are confused needs and motives in all of us, and there is always
an unspoken confusion between doing what is needed and
doing this work as an emblem of our own humanity. It's too
tempting to simply work each day to the point of exhaustion
and not take a critical look.

As we work we should be training ourselves out of a job,
making the refugees independent as rapidly as possible. Without a written document it's hard to teach or standardize care,
or to keep priorities in focus. I've been writing for several days,
and Donna and I stay up together each night revising the draft.
What a pity the medical care guidelines developed in Somalia
four years ago have not been provided.

March 12

Joan is off in Wad Medani for a few days' rest, and Tom and
Candy are back from Khartoum. They have decided to stay. In
Joan's absence I made rounds in the hospital.

I admitted to the hospital a 30-year-old man who had a
high fever and was in a coma. I tried to do a spinal tap to see
if he had meningitis but failed because I only had a needle
we use for injections. The needle was too short. I couldn't
reach the spinal canal. So I treated him for both meningitis and cerebral malaria at the same time. He looked near
death, and both diseases were possibilities. He died four hours
later. The women in the family who had been crowded around
the bed began crying and wailing. They left the ward waving
their arms in the air. The men tied his arms across his chest,
closed his mouth, and wrapped him in a thin white shroud.
The funeral was held just outside the ward. Then they carried

the body to the graveyard, which is about 150 yards from the hospital, straight out in the open field. The men were in a group carrying my patient, and the women followed in a separate group about 10 yards behind. I went outside and watched. I took a few pictures and felt dizzy in the 115-degree heat.

Tonight we had a pot luck "dinner party" at Fau 2 for the expatriates of Fau 1, 2, and 3. The people from Fau 1 did not show up, and we heard that two of them are sick. We sat outside in the dark on two creaking rope beds. The lantern went out, and no one cared enough to get up and find more fuel. Everyone looked tired and depressed.

March 13

It's near the end of my second week here, and finally I have some sense of productivity. Donna worked on organizing a better system of feeding the patients in the hospital, and I worked on the clinic. We roped off lines in the clinic and put up signs. *Nishtey* (children) get a special line so they will be seen first.

Sarah is out of camp, so I gave the daily lecture to the public health workers and organized a rotation system for them to work in the clinic as training.

Then I collected the new list of tents blown down to give to Abdulmonim. There were only a few tents on the list. On days like today that are still and hot, miniature tornadoes, called dust devils, spin through camp. If the tent is fastened tightly, it rips apart; otherwise it just blows away.

In the afternoon I went to the feeding center. I examined about twenty children, but I'm most concerned about Halima Mariam, a frail 4-year-old girl who is cared for by her 9-year-old sister. She is again refusing to eat.

I saw her in the clinic last week and admitted her to the hospital. Then she had diarrhea, was losing weight, and refusing to eat. She is one of the children who is less than 60 percent of her predicted weight. In the hospital Joan put a feeding tube into her stomach, and force-fed her for several days. I saw Halima in the hospital with the tube coming out of her nose. It was taped to her forehead with black electrician's tape, the only kind we have left.

Then I saw her three days ago, and she looked bright and was eating. Halima was released from the hospital, and her sister started bringing her back here to the feeding center. It looked like Joan's stubborn determination had saved this small girl.

Now Halima has a cough. Maybe she has pneumonia, but I doubt it because her lungs sounded clear. She may just have bronchitis, an infection in her upper airways. Without an X ray we can't really know.

These severely malnourished children are fussy eaters. They seem to lose interest in food. A sore mouth, an ear infection, or any other trivial illness, and they refuse to eat. To save them requires persistence and hard work. You have to reacquaint their shattered bodies with the will to live. Halima has no reserve. She can't afford to lose any more weight. She has to go back into the hospital and again be force-fed with a tube.

These children are so fragile. They are the sickest group in the camp. A doctor from the Centers for Disease Control (CDC) did a survey at Fau 2 last month and found that in only two weeks, 72 children died, out of 418 registered for therapeutic feeding. Parents bring the children to the clinic for an injection, but don't bring them to the feeding center. It's a fight to try and feed them all day long. The parents don't realize that injections and pills are useless if the children don't eat. Some of the children are so weak they need to be carried, and the parents aren't well enough to do this, or they live too far away. The children get quiet and apathetic and are easily ignored. We are not doing an adequate job with the malnourished kids: Less than half of the total number of severely malnourished children in the camp regularly come to therapeutic feeding.

In the clinic I sit with four refugees in training. No matter

(page 58)
Woman in the hospital,
Fau 3 refugee camp,
March 1985.

(page 59)
Fau 3 refugee camp, March
1985. Hospital.

what the complaint, I make them check each child's upper arm or thigh to look for wasting. The clinic has been rearranged so mothers and children sit inside on long wooden benches where they can see what is going on. I say over and over: Malnutrition is the worst disease, food is the best medicine. I've learned the Tigrinyan words *a bila eyo* (feed him), which I repeat to mothers holding the thin limbs of their infants. Sometimes I pick up a child and show the other mothers. I pantomime how strong the child will get if he eats, and the crowd of children and mothers laugh. I'm oblivious to how ridiculous my acting may appear. I want them to remember what I say.

Late at night Donna and I were still up working on the medical care guidelines, when a truck rolled in with twenty-nine sacks of CSM (corn-soy-milk powder) for the feeding center. One by one, everybody already in bed came out to see what was going on. We discovered that the truck also had another thirty-two huge cases containing Ritz crackers, courtesy of the government of Japan. I wonder who decided we need so many Ritz crackers. For a few minutes we made tired cynical jokes about evening cocktail parties for the refugees and about English butlers with silver trays serving the children their malnutrition porridge on Ritz crackers.

March 14

Everyone is losing weight. Sarah, Tom, and Joan blame their poor appetites on the heat, but there are probably psychological reasons as well that come from the constant contact with so much starvation and misery. Our food is so limited that I suspect last night's Ritz crackers are going to become a major item.

In the morning, Eiosis, our cook, sits down with a pan of dried lentil beans and patiently begins flipping them up in the air, again and again, each time uncovering another twig or pebble. She is usually at work when I leave for clinic in the morning, and sometimes still at work flipping the lentil beans when I return to the compound for lunch. Eventually she boils them or boils potatoes as an alternative. The afternoon is spent making a small mound of finely chopped onion, red pepper, and garlic, which is fried in oil and put on top of the boiled vegetable as spice. This has been dinner almost every night: boiled lentils or boiled potatoes.

In the last few nights I've started to cook, and Eiosis and I cook together. She regards my combinations (like frying eggplant and tomatoes and garlic and pepper together—and then putting it on top of spaghetti) as crazy. She laughs or shakes her head or waves her arms when she thinks I'm going completely beyond the bounds. We have no common language. When I discovered that she speaks a little Italian, I tried to speak to her in Spanish, hoping we would hit an occasional mutually understandable word. The effort was useless, and we both soon gave up. Now we just talk back and forth without regard, Eiosis in Tigrinyan and I in English.

March 15

Among all the sick and malnourished in the clinic today were two lively healthy kids who had stuck beans in their ears while playing. Shimelesh, one of the examiners, tried to irrigate them out without success. No head mirror. No bayonet forceps. I tried to hook one of the beans with a bent needle without luck. When I went back in the afternoon I brought superglue and put some on the tip of a wooden Q-tip but it wouldn't stick to the bean. So much for that advertisement about lifting a piano. I couldn't think of anything else to do, so I told the parents to bring them back in a week. (A week later the beans had dried out and shrunk, and I was able to remove them with our clumsy forceps.)

After I got back to the compound, someone brought a note

from Donna asking me to come help with a kid who seemed to have a broken arm. While walking back I was hoping that the kid had dislocated his shoulder and not broken his arm. I can diagnose a shoulder dislocation without X rays, and it's easy to put back in place. When I got to the ward I found the kid heavily drugged, almost in a coma. Donna had meant for the kid to have a teaspoon (5 ml.) of sedative by mouth. What he had received was the same volume by *injection,* which is ten times as powerful as the oral dose. Similar errors probably happen every day. The staff is untrained, overburdened, does not speak English, and in these circumstances it is impossible for us to adequately supervise and explain.

The child's arm was not deformed, but the middle of it was very tender and there was a lot of swelling. I put on a plaster splint and asked that the child stay on the ward for the next two days so we could watch him. (The next day when I came by to check he was gone. I never saw or heard about him again.)

After dinner Donna and I sat up working on the medical care guidelines by the light of a kerosene lantern. When she reached for her backpack, which she had set on the ground in the corner, she got stung by a scorpion. Squeezing her right hand she screamed in pain. I injected her finger with Xylocaine for the pain.

March 16

For the last two days we have been out of chloroquine, ampicillin, Flagyl, tetracycline, Septra, and penicillin. We can give only oral rehydration fluids to patients with dysentery. With only this treatment some of the weaker children may not survive. The director of the pharmacy is a political refugee from another camp, Tenedba. He is a very serious, conscientious man, and he speaks English in a dignified formal manner.

He has been in Sudan for five years and worked for IRC as a pharmacist at Tenedba.

He and I have a routine. "Doctor . . ." he begins haltingly, "I must have a moment of your time to bring to your attention a most urgent matter." He then presents me with the list of needed supplies. As I glance down the list, he gravely reads it out loud, usually with the same comment—"finished"—after each item. "Penicillin: finished . . . sticking plaster: finished . . . Septra liquid: finished . . . Septra tablets: finished." I thank him for bringing the needs to my attention and tell him I will do what I can. There is actually little that I can do. In between patients Donna keeps track of supplies, which is equivalent to supervising a large hospital pharmacy. She sends in the drug requests to the United Nations High Commissioner for Refugees (UNHCR) for shipments that are delivered every two weeks, but it doesn't seem to matter what we request. They send us what is available, dividing it up fairly between all the different camps. No one gets all that is needed. If we are particularly desperate we can go to Fau 2 or Fau 1 and try to borrow, but the most commonly used medicines are in short supply everywhere.

Yesterday in the pharmacy Donna found small amounts of everything being saved. Above her rising incredulous voice, I heard our dignified pharmacist vainly protesting that those medications were being saved "just in case." "In case of *what*?" asked Donna. "But . . . Doctor Donna . . . in case of an emergency!"

March 17

There's an epidemic of scurvy in Fau 3. It's been unrecognized, in front of our eyes. Several days ago we talked about the many patients with strange arthritis, patients crippled with painful swollen knees or painful ankles. Donna tried treating them with aspirin and noticed it didn't seem to work. Wasn't it a pity, she said, that we didn't have stronger arthritis medicines that are available in the United States. This morning three patients, almost back to back, came into the clinic with nosebleeds (a possible sign of scurvy). All three had swollen bleeding gums (a classic sign of scurvy). One of the patients also had knee pain. Finally, the diagnosis was apparent.

Scurvy is caused by lack of vitamin C and leads to fragility of the tiniest blood vessels. The patients tend to bleed, but often in a way that is hidden. This strange arthritis that we have been misdiagnosing is caused by bleeding about the weight-bearing joints, bleeding that occurs under the lining of the bones. Aspirin increases bleeding, only making the problem worse.

We checked our supply of vitamin C in the pharmacy and found that we have enough to distribute to the entire camp. The public health workers will give every refugee a 200 mg. pill of vitamin C twice a week, and we will send an urgent message to the central pharmacy for more. (With mass distribution of vitamin C scurvy disappeared from Fau 3. Workers in Fau 2 were not convinced that all this arthritis was from scurvy, and they did not mass distribute in their camp for several more weeks, until the scurvy in Fau 2 got even worse.)

On the way home I stopped for a visit at the REST compound. Their tent has no ventilation, and after two cups of tea I was dripping with sweat. I explained that I will start giving medical classes in the afternoons and hope to get treatment guidelines translated into Tigrinyan. Araya, one of the REST leaders, works with me in the clinic. He's in his early twenties, handsome and forceful, with a natural sense of authority. Arriving at the clinic before anyone else each morning, he stays without a break. I asked him what he thought about all of us starting clinic an hour earlier, at 6:30 A.M., because of the heat. He agrees it will be a good idea, and tomorrow we will change.

(opposite)
Fau 3 refugee camp, March 1985. Therapeutic Feeding Center.

Most of the time we just sat there together drinking tea and not talking, because we have very few words in common. I will keep visiting so they get to know me. They need confidence that IRC is interested in working with them.

March 18

A dusty wind blew all night. I slept poorly and had a nightmare about snakes. The guards have killed two of them this week. They were brown, about two feet long, with a triangular head: some type of poisonous vipers, either night adders or baby puff adders. Then last evening as we sat in the kitchen enclosure, another identical snake crawled between our chairs.

Work was long and hectic. An elderly man, Godamu Geberselassie, was carried into the clinic on a stretcher by two men. I looked down at my paper to write his name, and when I looked up they were covering him with a blanket. He died before I even had a chance to figure out how to spell his name. Sick and separated from his family and village in the move from Tukulubab, he had lain uncared for in a tent. (Later, I learned that he was one of the fifty-four old people on Sarah Barr's list.)

Shimelesh, one of our examiners, is now out sick after asking for vacation for the last two days. At work today he started vomiting and collapsed on the ground with a shaking chill. He has malaria. Joan is also sick. When I get up at night I hear her cough. Last night at 1:00 A.M. I gave her some medicine for the cough so she could get back to sleep. She has had a fever off and on, and she has been ignoring simple things like watching what water she drinks and washing her hands before she eats. Tom again has dysentery.

Last night Sarah Barr shaved her head. She had to convince us that she really wanted to do it before we would help. We all took turns, first cutting her hair short with my bandage scissors, and then shaving her scalp with a razor blade and soap. She joked and said that she had always wanted to do it. She said she "needed a change." This morning, when Sarah went into camp, the refugee women were horrified. They immediately understood. Her shaved head is a sign of intense grief. For me it is also an image of cancer, of chemotherapy and impending doom. But Sarah has too much vitality for the image to rest on her alone. We all helped shave her head, and it is a symbol for us as a group.

March 19

An epidemiologist is here from the CDC in Atlanta, surveying the health problems here and in other camps. He gave us two boxes of U.S. Army C rations. The gift made us feel giddy, like an unexpected Christmas. Five of us sat down and divided up small cans of tuna, franks and beans, cheese, and chocolate.

We talked with the epidemiologist about the lack of medical leadership from the Sudanese or UNHCR and how costly this has been in the entire program of relief. We told him about running out of chlorine, and how futile it was treating diarrhea and then letting refugees drink the same foul water.

He said that the Sudanese are worried that the refugees will somehow pollute the water supply even worse, and he told us a bizarre story about the top health official, who is preoccupied with the amount of feces the refugees produce. At a recent health-policy meeting, the official described the amount of stool that an entire camp will produce in a day or a week or a month, calculating from the volume of stool one adult produces in a day. The astounding figures were put forth for debate, ignoring that the refugees defecate in fields away from the water, where the waste rapidly dries and only fertilizes the fields.

The epidemiologist says that the initial weekly death rate in Fau 3 is the highest that he has ever seen, one and a half times the death rate in the worst Cambodian refugee camp at the worst time. In less than two months more than 3 percent of the camp population has died—505 people, mostly children. He says that starvation during the civil war in Biafra in 1969–70 was also quite severe, but the data from there is fragmentary. If the epidemiologist is right, perhaps the all-time world record belongs to Fau 3.

March 20

As I walked home from the clinic, an agitated refugee woman confronted me. She reached into a sack and brought out a handful of grain. She thrust her hand out at me, as if to say "Look at this! Look at this!" I did not have the vaguest idea what was wrong. It turns out that the ration has been distributed unmilled.

Abdulmonim explained that one thousand sacks of dura arrived unmilled and there are no stones in the area to grind it. The grain is inedible if not milled. Two mills that are supposed to be at this camp have not yet been built, and the one at Fau 2 is broken. Abdulmonim sent the dura back to Gedaref, which had the only mill large enough to grind the dura in time for distribution. He says it was sent back—still unmilled—with a "very severe note." He didn't tell us what the note said, but I suspect he was berated. The Sudanese are having their own difficulties, and he tells me that there has been no electricity most of the week in Gedaref.

And yesterday the UNHCR field officer for the Fau camps told us that the ration will probably be reduced. There is word that one hundred thousand more refugees from Ethiopia are "in the pipeline" to Sudan. UNHCR fears that food will run out. This comes on top of last week's news from the UNHCR nutritionist that we are losing ground with the malnourished kids.

Jessica Sanders arrived yesterday. Born in Kenya and raised in Africa and the United States, she worked with Sarah Barr in Somalia, and she also worked in Lebanon. She is a

(opposite)
Fau 3 refugee camp, March 1985. A child in the Therapeutic Feeding Center is gaining weight.

(page 70)
The hospital, Fau 3 refugee camp, noon, March 12, 1985. A woman learns that her husband has died suddenly of meningitis.

poised, tall quiet woman with short hair. Her high voice rises even more at the end of sentences, in an African cadence. Her parents are missionaries here in Sudan, and although she was brought over by IRC to work in the camps, her services have already been requested by both UNHCR and the Sudanese Ministry of Health. She has spoken to people in Khartoum about those jobs and felt she ought to come to Fau 3 before deciding what job to take. She came with no luggage, so I wasn't optimistic about her staying.

This evening Jessica announced in her funny voice that it seems she's most needed here at Fau 3. She asked Sarah if she could borrow some clothes, so she can stay in camp and start work right away. She will have her things sent out from Khartoum.

March 22

A meningitis epidemic has broken out. Although nobody says it out loud, we are all frightened. Meningococcal meningitis is one of the very few infections that can kill a healthy adult in a matter of hours. It can usually be cured with antibiotics, but every doctor has seen cases impossible to control. Medicine textbooks have pictures of these patients, with hemorrhages scattered over the skin and black gangrene of the arms and legs. The disease is highly contagious. During epidemics many people carry the infection in their throats and spread it without themselves getting sick. Only Donna has been vaccinated. In hospitals at home, a meningitis patient would immediately be placed in an isolation room in the intensive care unit. We would be required to put on protective gown, mask, and gloves before going into the room. The Sahel is called the "meningitis belt" of Africa. This region is notorious for large uncontrollable epidemics.

I saw three cases in the clinic this morning, and one of the people has already died. A few days ago, after the first case, we sent word that we have an emergency. We urgently need to vaccinate the entire camp, but there has been no word yet about when we get vaccine. The message is going to be relayed again by a Danish emergency field coordinator for UNHCR.

By chance he drove up to the ward as I walked out with a syringe of spinal fluid in my hand. I had just done a spinal tap and was walking to the hut where we keep the microscope. He greeted me and innocently asked how things were going. I showed him the sample. Spinal fluid should be crystal clear, and this sample looked like pus. I explained what was happening. He appreciates the problem. His son became deaf from meningitis last year.

At 5:00 P.M., when I finished teaching in the clinic, I went back to the hospital. Outside were several stretchers and numerous other people wrapped up in blankets lying on the ground. Donna and I examined each person and found one with meningitis. Some of the rest were sick with other illnesses, and all of them were hysterical.

This epidemic has captured the imagination of the entire camp. As I walked back to our compound, I realized that today has brought us a glimpse of the middle ages. I can sense in the air the same clutch of terror people felt during the legendary epidemics of the past.

As if the epidemic weren't enough, we have continued to have a problem with snakes. Just after dark we saw one in the shower. Later Jessica spotted one in Donna's *tukul;* and Musa, our driver, was bitten while trying to kill it. He was swinging at it wildly with a stick, and he flipped it up in the air between us. The snake must have grazed Musa's shoulder as it came down. We could barely see the bite marks, which looked like two tiny skin breaks on his shoulder.

At first we couldn't imagine that much venom could have gotten in, and we did not give Musa antitoxin. I gave him a codeine pill, and Donna put a special black rock over the bite. This is a folk remedy for snakebite, given to Donna by a missionary friend from southern Sudan. Two hours later Musa's shoulder was very swollen, and he was in severe pain. We finally treated him with antitoxin.

When I checked on him just after midnight he was sitting up, afraid that if he fell asleep he would die. I reassured him, and he went to sleep. Abdulmonim told me that in these parts the usual treatment for snakebite is to immediately cut off the finger or toe that is bitten.

March 23

My day began with watching Donna throw her flashlight and come to the verge of tears. Just after sunrise she'd spotted another snake in her *tukul*. This time we pinned the snake down with a stick before striking at the head. Musa, who now feels fine, was delighted with this improvement in our technique, and he enthusiastically helped with the kill.

Arriving in the clinic at 6:30 A.M., I immediately sent five more people with meningitis to the hospital. I found them lying under the shelter wrapped in blankets. They had high fevers and necks so rigid I could lift each person up like a board. With cases like this we no longer bother performing a spinal tap.

At 11:00 A.M. I went to the town of El Fau with Abdulmonim, the IRC medical director, and the IRC administrator for the Fau camps. We went to the local hospital to alert the Sudanese health authorities about the meningitis outbreak and to see if they have any meningitis vaccine. We also needed to replenish our supply of snake antitoxin.

(opposite)
Fau 3 refugee camp,
March 18, 1985. Godamu
Geberselassie died in the
clinic before I even had a
chance to figure out how to
spell his name.

After telling them why we came, they insisted we have a meeting. We waited. Finally we gathered in the office of Hussein Tahrir, a lawyer who is commissioner for the regional agricultural project, and, apparently, the local political boss. Nine of us were present. The meeting immediately degener-

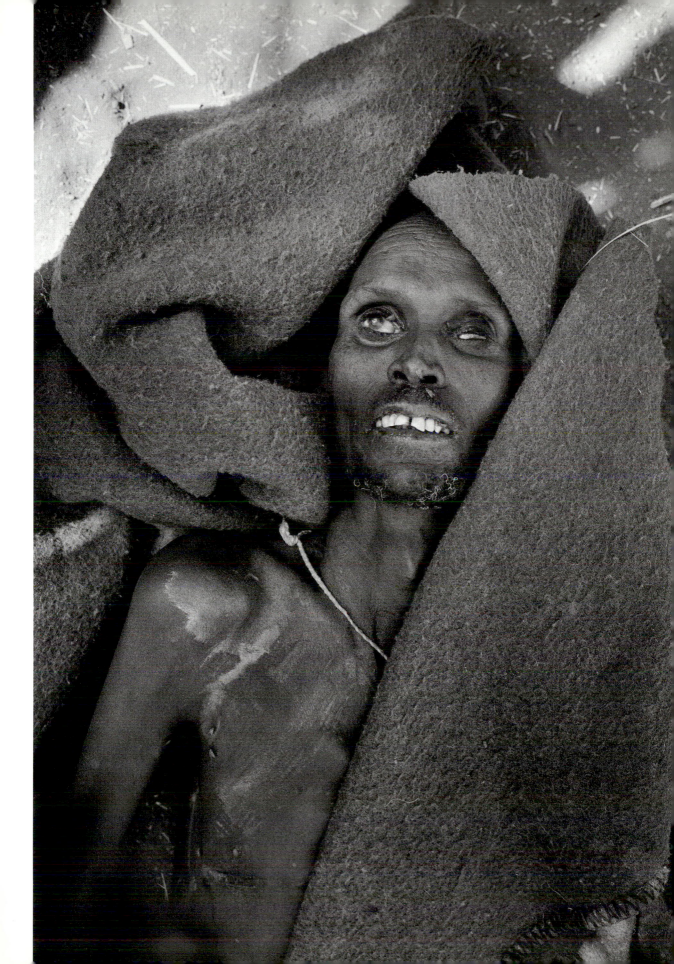

ated into five people gesturing and shouting in Arabic at the same time.

The public health officer for the town of El Fau said he had some vaccine, but when we went to his office we discovered that he only had the fluid used to dilute the vaccine, not the vaccine itself. We did have luck with snake antitoxin and got another four vials. Hussein Tahrir offered to take me tomorrow morning to Wad Medani, the capital of the Blue Nile region, where we have been assured there is vaccine.

And today Joan Porter's tour of duty came to an end. We noticed that her eyes are yellow. She has hepatitis and will go home.

Joan's last words before we drove off to El Fau this morning were, "What should I do about preventive medicine for meningitis? Should I take the medicine with my liver? Yesterday I accidentally sprayed some spinal fluid from a patient up my nose . . ." Joan needed preventive medicine once before. She had been working in a hospital in Alaska and had kissed a sick baby in her care. The infant had died of unsuspected meningitis six hours later. After that incident Joan had taken Rifampin as a preventive medicine, and the drug had dangerously inflamed her liver.

We decided that the safest medicine would be a large dose of penicillin by vein. On a mattress on the floor of my *tukul*, Sarah and I started an intravenous line on Joan and gave her five million units of penicillin by vein.

March 24

At 7:00 last night, as she walked out of the shower, Donna stepped on a snake. She started screaming hysterically. The bite was severe, and she needed antitoxin. I had to grab her in a bear hug to get her down on the cot in the middle of our compound. We had the equipment together, and we were practiced from treating Musa the night before. Donna wanted everything, including the black rock on her foot and for Jessica to hold her hand and pray. We treated her by lantern light and then by the headlights of the car. After the antitoxin we decided to go to the hospital at El Fau in case she needed a blood transfusion. I ducked into my *tukul* to grab some things, and at the edge of the flashlight beam saw a scorpion disappear under my bed.

Four of us slept together in one of the rooms in the hospital at El Fau. Another short and gritty night's sleep. I dreamed that I was back in San Francisco and that a close friend had died. I pictured him looking like one of the emaciated refugees, and for some reason I waited before going to visit. He died before I saw him, and I woke up startled to find myself in a hospital bed in El Fau.

I stayed with Donna until she could be taken to Wad Medani. Another IRC person will drive her from Wad Medani to a hospital in Khartoum. Donna's leg is swollen to the knee and very painful. We have been visited steadily since 7 A.M. by a stream of exotic veiled Sudanese women who enter in large, shy groups. I presume they must be the hospital nurses. They speak no English, walk in, smile, shake hands, and then leave. Hussein Tahrir visited at 6:00 A.M. and said he would be back midmorning, when Donna is supposed to be picked up, to take me to Wad Medani for meningitis vaccine.

7:00 P.M.

I spent the afternoon with Hussein Tahrir, but I'm not sure if we were searching for vaccine or chasing the African wind. We looked for him from midmorning and could not track him down in any of the places we were supposed to meet him or were told to find him.

At 1:00 P.M. Hussein Tahrir appears. "We must hurry," he says. "Things close at 2:00 P.M." I assume he is referring to the place to get vaccine. Wad Medani is about an hour's car trip away. He drives like a madman but still stops to pick up

(page 78)
Fau 3 refugee camp,
5:00 P.M., March 22, 1985.
A suspected meningitis
victim is found on the
ground in front of the
hospital.

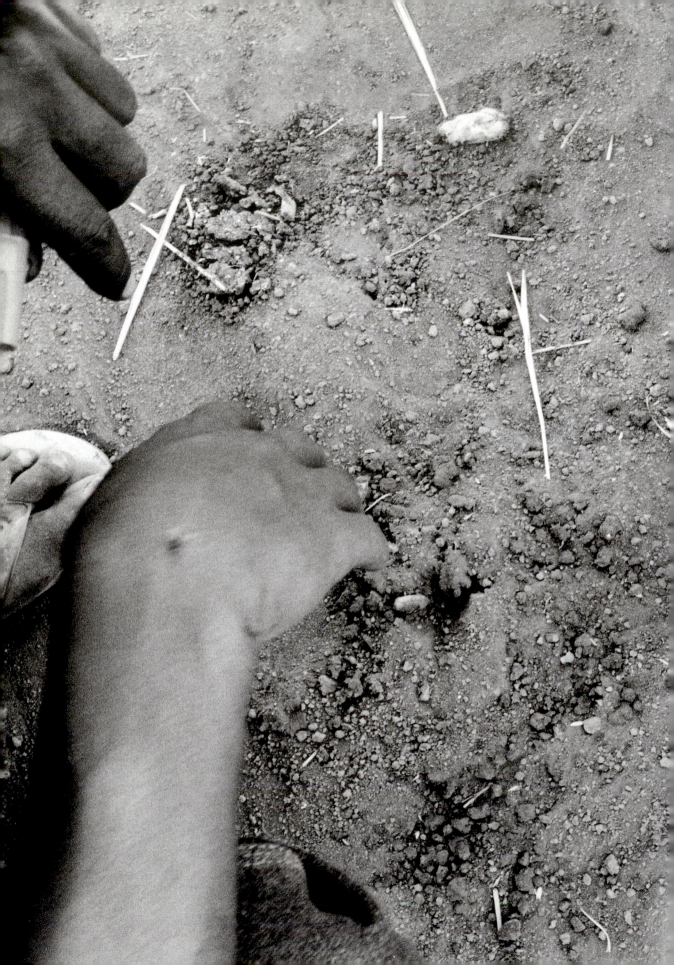

two hitchhikers, because "it is the Moslem way." We arrive at Wad Medani just before 2:00 P.M.

We go straight to the video store. Then to the duty-free shop. So the afternoon goes: errand after errand, a stop for lunch, a bath, prayer. At each stop he does inquire about the vaccine, or so he tells me. All conversation is in Arabic, which I don't understand. Finally all his errands are done, and we go to the hospital, checking in four different places without luck. Then we are sent to a doctor's house, and he is not home. We are directed to the clinic. The doctor is not there, and the clinic is closed. By late afternoon we find ourselves at the home of the minister of health for the entire Blue Nile region. His daughter welcomes us in and then disappears. She is back fifteen minutes later with cold lemonade and again disappears. Twenty minutes later she is back to announce that her father is not at home, but that I can find him at eight the next morning at his office in the Ministry of Health. She gives me directions how to get there. Hussein Tahrir says there is nothing more I can do until morning, and we return to the Suks because he still has more shopping. He then leaves me and returns to El Fau. I confess to myself that I had a great time.

March 25

MORNING, WAD MEDANI

At 8:00 A.M. I am sitting in the empty office of the Minister of Health, Blue Nile Region. Then it is 9:00 A.M. Someone comes in and says "in a half an hour he will arrive." Finally I speak with the minister, who is extremely cordial. "This is very serious," he says. "I must call in my health advisor." After another thirty minutes, in comes Dr. Oman, a very distinguished older man with white hair. We are served tea. I repeat the story of our meningitis epidemic to Dr. Oman and say that we urgently need vaccine. He immediately agrees. "It is best if we send a whole team with trained personnel, equipment, *and* vaccine," he says. I emphasize that we need help right away, and Dr. Oman says, "How about tomorrow?"

"Great," I say, "but can I have at least some vaccine to take back today? At least enough to immunize our medical staff."

"I will give you a driver and send you directly over to the director of immunization bearing my letter of request," he responds.

He scribbles a note in Arabic for me. I felt like I was about to win the grand prize in an international scavenger hunt. While the driver from the Ministry of Health took me across town, I was thinking about how many doses to insist on and how I could be certain to keep the vaccine cold enough to keep its potency. Besides keeping us from catching meningitis, bringing back the vaccine would be a vital boost to morale.

I arrived at the vaccination headquarters and presented my note to the appropriate official. He seemed indifferent and bored:

"We have no vaccine in Wad Medani," he said. "We will send your request to Khartoum. We will notify your public health officer to make arrangements when it comes." ◇

Snakes and meningitis were like twin gargoyles, boundary marks that showed we had reached the bottom. Donna was picked up in Wad Medani and taken, with Joan, to the hospital in Khartoum. Vaccine promised for two days before had still not arrived at Fau, and we couldn't get a straight answer from the regional office of UNHCR in Gedaref. We had been told that an emergency supply for Fau 3 was being flown from Khartoum. After taking Joan and Donna to the hospital, our driver promised to go directly to the Ministry of Health and check. When I arrived back at Fau 3 midday March 25, our administrator screamed at me for leaving the camp.

We had reached our collective limit. The isolation, bad

food, desolate landscape, insufferable level of misery and illness, lack of supplies, overwork, and frustration had taken a large physical and emotional toll.

I found Candy McDonald alone in the compound sitting on her bed. She was unable to work, emotionally paralyzed, convinced that she was going to die of meningitis in Fau 3. Like Candy, the rest of us were all afraid. Sarah Barr had already shaved off all her hair, and her eyes were a mess with a bad infection, probably trachoma. She morosely stalked the camp, a tall handsome woman with a bald head and red eyes. She trained the entire group of public health workers in the proper way to apply antibiotic eye ointment by having them practice on her eyes.

It was now that we got forms from the New York office asking us to "evaluate our experience." Tom McDonald, who'd been sick a whole week each month with dysentery, said, "The only thing I feel would be right to do with this silly paper is to wipe my rear end with it and send it along."

(page 84)
*Fau 3 refugee camp, March
1985. Man trying to warm
himself in the
early-morning sun.*

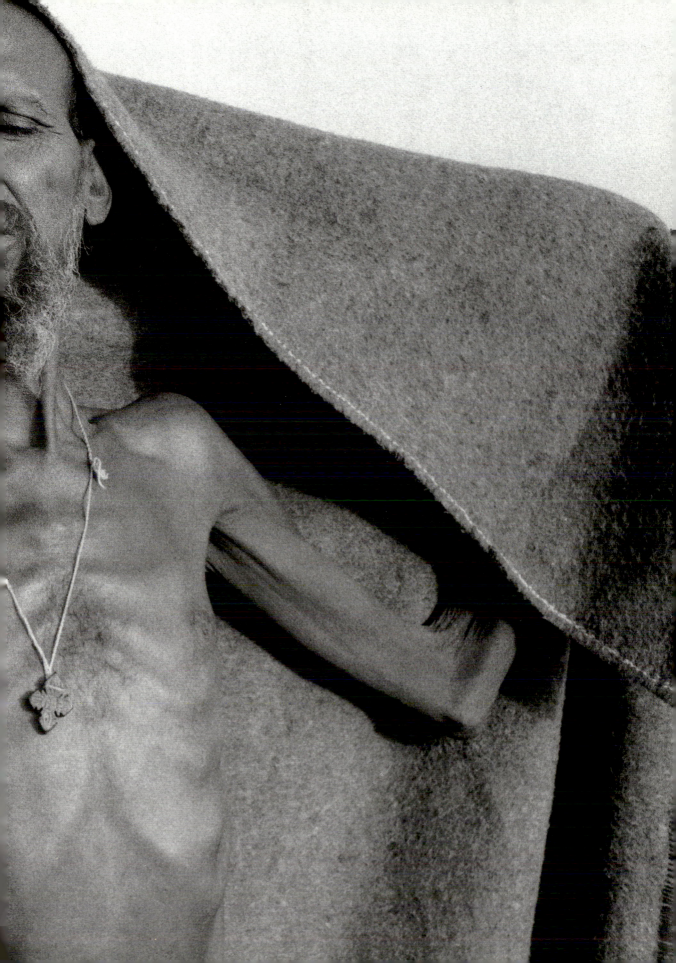

CONTROL AT A PRICE
Fau 3 Refugee Camp,
March 25–April 20, 1985

(opposite)
Fau 3 refugee camp,
March 26, 1985. A child
that has just received his
vaccine for meningitis.

March 25, evening

The vaccine arrived just a few minutes after I got back to Fau 3. Sarah and I scouted where to set up immunization. By 3:00 P.M. her public health workers had organized lines of people getting shots.

I went behind the hospital to the meningitis ward. Donna set it up three days ago, in the small thatch shack she was having built for maternity care. The new ward is filled. The roof is so low there are places where it's impossible to stand, and the room has a fearful mood that is different from the hospital, clinic, or feeding center. It feels like the quietest place in camp. Several of the patients are in a coma. There are few family members and little interaction between patients and family or nurses. We've put the ward under quarantine. Guards stand just inside the doorway in the shade.

I found Brian Cole examining a patient, and I introduced myself. He's an exuberant medical resident who arrived in Sudan two weeks ago to work as a doctor at Fau 1. Yesterday he transferred over to Fau 3 to replace Joan and Donna. He says that for the last two days meningitis patients were still coming in—often draped over crude log stretchers. "Sick on a stick," Brian calls them.

March 26

Last night Brian Cole told us how he needed to exercise each day before going to work. This morning when I left for the hospital he was jumping rope to Bruce Springsteen and "Born in the U.S.A." Then he got violently sick with dysentery. He spent the day in the latrine, or lying in my hammock. He was so dehydrated that Tom started an intravenous line and gave him two liters of fluids by vein. I don't suppose he will work for another few days.

I have another mild bout of diarrhea, but I feel okay. I

thought to myself, as I was trying to keep my balance while squatting in the latrine in wilting heat in the middle of a cloud of flies: When I get home I am not going to really believe this happened. It has been so awful. I'll imagine it was just a bad dream.

March 27

I may have killed a child this morning with an injection of chloroquine. He was 5 years old, with a high fever and continuous seizures. He had either cerebral malaria or meningitis. I couldn't do a spinal tap while he was having a seizure. I gave him injections of antibiotic, chloroquine, and medicine for the seizures. I stood there for a few minutes with his mother and father trying to think of something else I could do, something I might have overlooked. A list of measures ran through my mind that might help the child, but none can be done in this camp. Then I walked over to the clinic.

I was examining my second patient when a nurse called me back to the ward. Fifteen minutes after my medicines the child stopped breathing and died.

March 28

The epidemiologist from the CDC is back to help us track our meningitis epidemic. The medical director of IRC is also here. I told him that I can't stay in Fau 3 much longer, that I'm close to my limit. In a few more weeks, after meningitis is under control, I'll have to get away from this place.

We've talked about abandoning the IRC compound at Fau 3 and finding a house for the team at Ashra, a nearby Sudanese village. Meanwhile, I've been sleeping over at Fau 2, at the UNHCR compound, so I don't have to walk around the Fau 3 compound at night. It's inconvenient, but I sleep better and have stopped having nightmares about snakes.

March 29

A cool beautiful black, moonless African night with brilliant stars from one horizon to the other. For several hours I lay on my back and watched, and finally, at 11:00 P.M., the entire curling tail of Scorpio was above the horizon.

March 30

Is this nightmare beginning to relent? Only one new case of meningitis today. I did a spinal tap on a second child with headache, lethargy, and high fever, and the spinal fluid was clear. The child probably just has malaria or typhoid fever.

We have all been working frantically to control the epidemic, and I have kept to myself this black feeling that nothing will work and things will continually get worse. In three days we have immunized the entire camp: almost thirteen thousand people. We have also given preventive antibiotics to all persons in the same tent as meningitis patients and in a ring of tents two deep.

There's a funny map of the camp in Abdulmonim's office, with pins for each tent that has had a case. There is no clustering or pattern. It looks like a high school science project where the experiment didn't work. What's different from high school is that when I look at Abdulmonim's map I see fifteen people with meningitis, and four people dead.

The epidemic has had a ripple effect. Children in the clinic are now terrified to be examined, because of their recent experience with immunization shots. Numerous adults are still brought in on stretchers complaining of stiff necks, frightened they have caught meningitis.

In the middle of work today, with our measures to control the epidemic finally in place, a pompous Sudanese bureaucrat visited to tell us how we should manage the epidemic:

"You must wash everything daily in a solution of half bleach and half water," he said, without realizing that there is no bleach in the camp.

"You must treat all cases with injections of triple sulfa antibiotic," he continued, quoting from a medical text that is thirty years out of date.

"You must instruct everyone in camp to sleep head to foot so they will not breathe in each other's faces and spread disease."

At first I tried to point out things that were not practical. He replied that he had the authority to insist on our following his exact instructions. I stopped arguing and said we would do our best. He had told me his name and title, which I immediately forgot, and it was too awkward to ask him again who he was.

Later, Abdulmonim said to me, "Please do not concern yourself about that visitor. He is merely being meddlesome. I doubt that we will ever see him again."

March 31

It's Sunday, and I got up before sunrise to go to Coptic Church services at a tent near our compound. Inside the tent, through an open seam, I watched a baptism. A tiny infant, just one week old, was reverently bathed in a chipped, white enamel bowl of water filled from a dented tin can for cooking oil. It was a euphoric moment for me to see this ritual celebrating the renewal of life amid all the misery and death.

I spent the rest of the day writing a detailed report on the month of March at Fau 3—what has happened and what needs to be done—and I finished just after dark. I have never spent a better day.

(page 92)
Fau 3 refugee camp,
March 31, 1985. Sunday
just after sunrise, Coptic
Church services are held at
a tent near our compound.

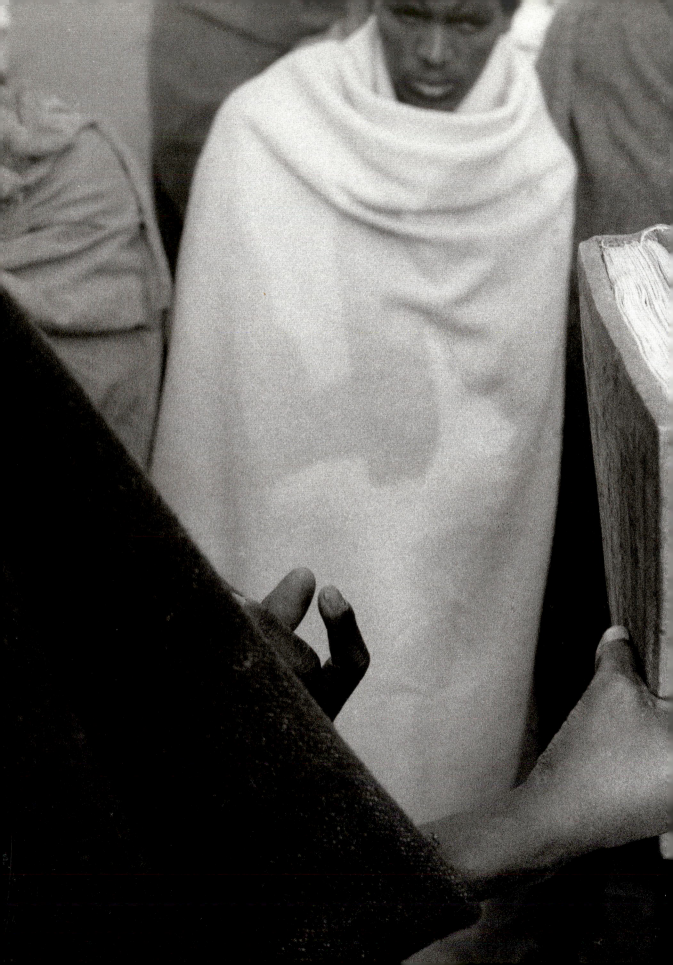

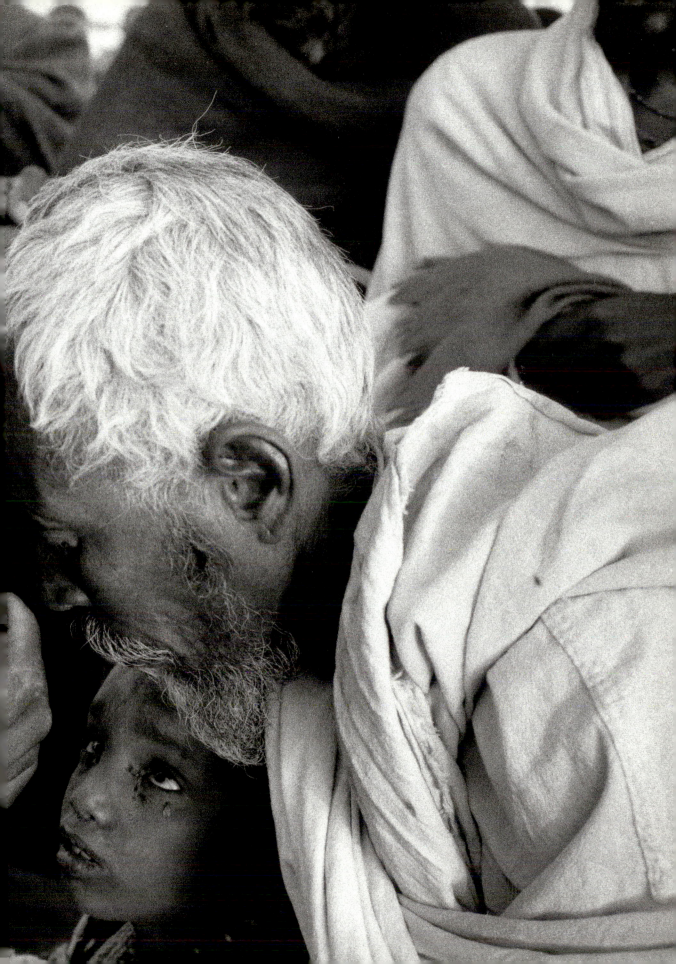

April 1

Religion is also compounding our problems. The women who are pregnant or breast feeding desperately need better nutrition. We are trying to give them milk each day in the feeding centers, but they are refusing the milk because it is Lent. First we tried to convince the women that in these circumstances it is a medicine and not a food, but that approach did not work. Then we met with the priests. They seemed unwilling to advise the women to drink milk or to temporarily consider milk a medicine. Finally we suggested that in the current circumstances there might be some way to be more forgiving. There was conversation, and the priests appeared to nod in sympathy. But the interpreter was incapable of translating their words, and I have no idea what was really understood.

April 2

Musa has a toothache. This morning he showed me, the right front tooth on top. As I was leaving for the clinic, Brian mentioned that maybe he'd help Musa out.

Five years ago I spent time working with the dentist at Khao I Dang, a refugee camp on the Thai-Cambodian border. Pulling teeth was harder than I had expected. You needed to understand the anatomy, where to give anesthetic, and what motions to use when you pull. You must have the right tools.

When I got back to the compound at lunchtime, all of Brian's buoyancy was gone. Musa was missing half his right front tooth. His lip and the entire right side of his face was ballooned up with infection. Brian gave him antibiotics, and this afternoon they will visit the local Sudanese dentist in the town of El Fau and get the remaining broken half tooth removed.

Sarah's organized her own farewell party for tonight. With the meningitis epidemic I think she's finally spent herself. This past week she led the public health team in a grueling non-stop effort. The epidemic now seems under control, and it's largely to their credit. They tracked down every single case and every contact, gave preventive medicines, organized the entire camp for immunization, and supervised giving vaccine. Jessica is taking over public health. Sarah is absolutely ready to leave, but the medical director has now begged her to stay one more week, and she agreed.

I was late going to the party, and walked into camp in the dark by myself. I made several photographs as I walked through camp. The refugees, who live in a world without electricity, were astounded by my flash attachment. Several teenage girls followed me, screaming and laughing at each startling burst of light.

The Therapeutic Feeding Center had been set up for the party. All the tables and chairs from the clinic, pharmacy, feeding center, and hospital were placed along the walls. The ceiling was hung with oil lanterns and the walls with paper decorations and signs. We danced on the dirt floor to Michael Jackson tapes in dim light that filtered through the dust. Two sheep, butchered this morning, were made into traditional spicy stew, and the special treat was Aragy, a fermented dates "moonshine" obtained from a still at Tenedba. It was served with Coca Cola but still tasted bitter and burned. Speeches of thanks to Sarah were made in Tigrinyan to applause and then translated. She was given a number of touching handmade presents, and Sarah smiled radiantly.

There was also a skit about someone with a stethoscope who kept stopping to take pictures.

April 4

Fights broke out in camp last night after the party, and today I was called to meet with Abdulmonim. Evidently there were several different incidents: Amharics fought among themselves, and a Tigrayan was jumped and beaten, probably by other Tigrayans. The Tigrayan has a broken jaw and a bone-deep cut next to his left eye. I sewed up the cut, but his jaw needs an operation. There's nothing I can do. The bone is displaced and needs to be put back and wired. He may have permanent trouble eating.

Abdulmonim is concerned about tension between the Amharics and Tigrayans. He sees two factors of importance: First, dates were distributed in the last ration, and he says these were fermented and distilled into Aragy. "The police tell me most of them were smelling," said Abdulmonim.

Second, he is concerned that the young Amharic men working for IRC have no women of their own. They are well paid and well dressed compared to the Tigrayan refugee men, who are literally in rags. "This can cause hot blood and very many problems, and these young men should stay out of the camp at night," he said.

He is annoyed that last night Sarah and Amy were there when he arrived with the police—and only with difficulty did he get them to leave. "If they stayed they would have become involved," he said. "The security police would have taken their names." He asked me to call a meeting of all the IRC staff to discuss these problems, and he asked me to advise my expatriate colleagues to keep away, "especially the females." He advised that political discussions be forbidden.

At 4:00 P.M. the staff met in the empty feeding center, the same place as last night's party. There were about eighty of us from the feeding centers, clinic, ward: Amharics, Tigrayans, and expatriates. The meeting was short but went slowly be-

cause everything had to be translated twice, into both Tigrinyan and Amharic.

First I announced that in the last three days there had been
no new cases of meningitis, and that I wished to congratulate
them all for their magnificent work in defeating the epidemic.
Everyone in the room clapped and shouted, and a few of the
women let out piercing tribal cries.

Then I came to the point. I announced the policies suggested by Abdulmonim: Amharic workers need to stay in their
tent area and out of camp at night. If there are any quarrels,
the police will immediately arrest them. Anyone found guilty
by the police must be fired and leave camp, without question
or appeal. Drinking alcohol is against the law of Sudan, and
if they have Aragy they should keep to their tents. Finally,
political discussions are forbidden.

I made certain that everything was clearly understood,
but fairness of the rules was, on purpose, not discussed. As I
walked back to our compound, I remembered my protest days
as a college student in the late 1960s, and wondered how I
had just now, without the slightest qualm, prohibited political
discussions.

April 5

Today I discharged the last meningitis patient from the hospital. It wasn't a happy scene. The child doesn't understand why
he is now deaf, and he cried unconsolably.

Even the environment seemed against us. The wind blew
continuously, 30 to 50 miles per hour, and everything was
covered with fine brown dust. All day I could feel the fine
grittiness between my teeth. To write anything I first had to
blow off the paper, but after two or three sentences it was
covered with dust again. Every few minutes there were more
violent gusts of wind. A heavy cloud of dust would blow right

(page 98)
Fau 3 refugee camp,
April 3, 1985. Butchering a
sheep for Sarah Barr's
farewell party.

through the clinic, stopping all work. People would cover their faces with a shirt or blanket, and while my head was wrapped up I would hear everyone coughing, and I would see them wiping their eyes after the dust had passed.

In the evening when I got home, I borrowed Amy's tape deck. Of the dozen tapes I brought with me, the only one I can listen to is a collection of Maria Callas arias from her great tragic operas. Tonight I came in exhausted, too tired to speak. The wind had finally quit. I listened to Maria Callas, and I looked out over an endless horizon into the magic African twilight.

Earlier, on my way back to the compound, all I felt like doing was lighting a huge bonfire. Burn our compound, or better still, burn the whole camp. Cauterize this entire spot on earth, I thought to myself, so this wound on humanity will scar over and this pain will abate.

After Maria Callas I feel that maybe the bonfire can wait until tomorrow.

April 6

Sudan has been one of the top stories on the BBC for the past week. Every evening we crowd around Jessica's radio while she searches through the static for the nightly news. President Gaafar Muhammed Nimieri is out of the country, and there have been riots in Khartoum. Mobs have turned over cars and broken windows in the hotels where Americans stay.

This morning Abdulmonim did not show up for the weekly camp coordination meeting. First we were told that he would just be a few minutes late. Then we were told that he has been called away. We have just gotten word that there has been a coup. Nimieri is deposed. We are saving two drums of petrol in each camp as emergency fuel. If we need to evacuate, the plan is to drive to Port Sudan and leave the country by boat.

I almost forgot that today is Easter. Musa, a Muslim,

bought a chicken for Eiosis as an Easter gift. Eiosis was over-joyed.

April 7

It's near the end of Sarah's last week. It was pointless for her to stay this extra week. She is exhausted, unable to work. I watch her and feel like I'm seeing someone who just survived a train crash or an earthquake. She walks around camp as if she is wandering among the wreckage, waiting for the scene to end.

Sarah is highly protective of all the people she has worked with, and today we had a fight after I fired a guard who comes from outside of the camp. IRC made a commitment to REST that all unskilled jobs would go to refugees that live in this camp, and REST came to me to complain.

Looking at Sarah I realize how much of this disaster I missed, and what a burden this experience will be to carry home. Fau 3 was already a month old when I arrived. She was here at the beginning, and also at Fau 1 when that camp opened, and at Fau 2.

But Fau 3 has been the worst, with snakes, meningitis, iso-lation, and the highest death rate of all. Is it possible that so much agony has been released into the world from this tiny desolate spot in only two months?

April 8

My head feels terrible. I'm sick again and so is Brian Cole. We have identical symptoms: ferocious headache, sore throat, fever, muscle ache. It's probably the same virus that Jessica is just getting over. I spent from 6:30 to 9:30 A.M. in the clinic, and the rest of the day inside my *tukul*. We closed the doors and windows, in an effort to make it dark and cool. The bril-liant sunlight hurts my eyes and vibrates through my head. I imagine myself in San Francisco, lying in my own bed, look-ing out at the soothing gray fog and listening to the mournful foghorns. Amy came in the *tukul* while Brian and I were lying in the hammocks half asleep.

"If Abdulmonim is going to castrate me and put me in a shroud I can't stay here," she announced with anger and bitterness. After the fights in camp a few nights ago, Abdul-monim declared that the translators' tents are off limits at night. At first Amy went along, but now she again wants to spend time there. She tells us that Nuur is teaching her Arabic and giving her music lessons.

Yesterday Amy skipped work. She and Nuur took the car and spent most of the day in a nearby village called Ashra try-ing to get somebody out of jail. She took off without checking with the rest of us, and we needed the car to carry supplies for the feeding center. Nuur was one of those arrested last week, in the fights after Sarah's party, and his friend is in the Ashra jail.

This brings back too many unpleasant memories about the kind of things that happen when we start forgetting why we've been sent here.

On my first trip, in Thailand, several people on our team ended up spending much of their time smuggling cigarettes and sugar into the Khao I Dang refugee camp for their trans-lators and friends. They tried to make smuggling a "team project."

"If I was a refugee I'd want cigarettes more than any-thing," one of my coworkers told me angrily when several of us refused to help. The ringleader, an acupuncturist from Berkeley, attacked me and the other doctor and accused us of acting superior, just because we were doctors, and of being "male chauvinists" who were unwilling to share in "team re-sponsibilities." They also tried to get us to write phony medi-cal letters to get their friends back and forth between camp and the Cambodian border. The four-room teak house where

*(opposite and page 104)
Fau 3 refugee camp, late afternoon, April 11, 1985. The woman needs a cesarean section, but it is impossible in the camp, and there is no way to transport her.*

*(pages 106 and 107)
Fau 3 refugee camp, early morning, April 12, 1985. At sunrise I find a happy mother and a perfect baby. In a nearby bed is a child with overwhelming infection, whose body temperature has now suddenly fallen below normal. With nothing left to try, I asked the father to use his own body to keep the child warm.*

*(page 108)
Fau 3 refugee camp, April 12, 1985. The father, moments after our efforts to save his child had failed.*

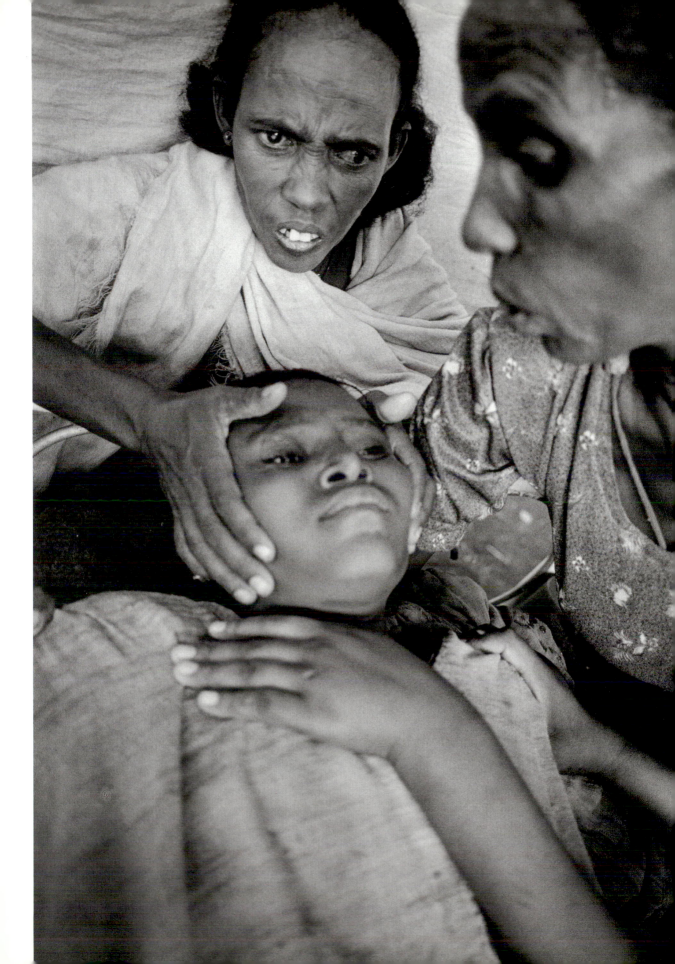

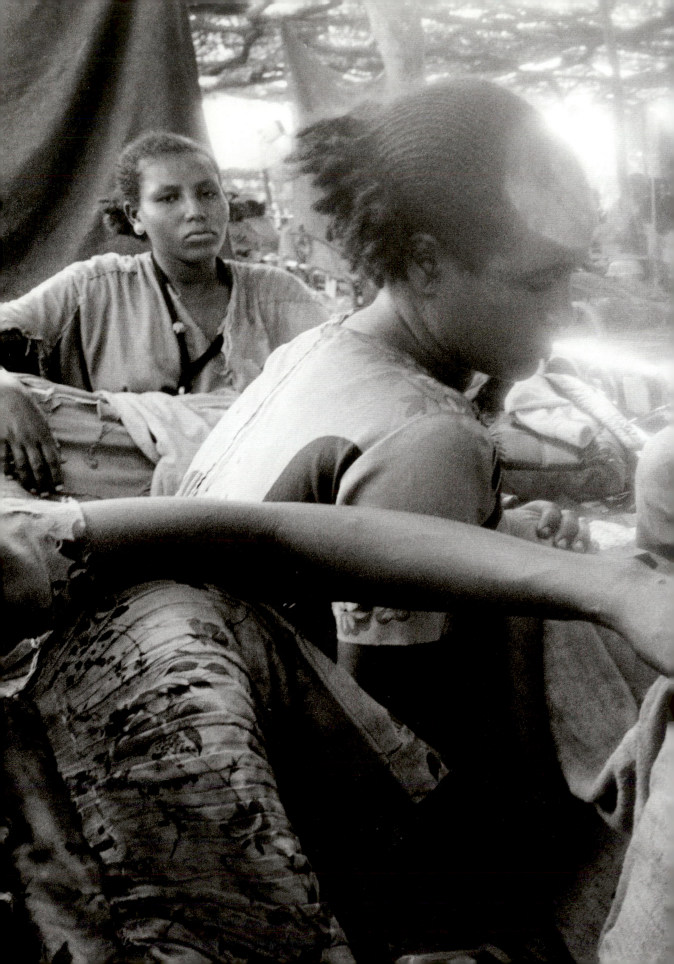

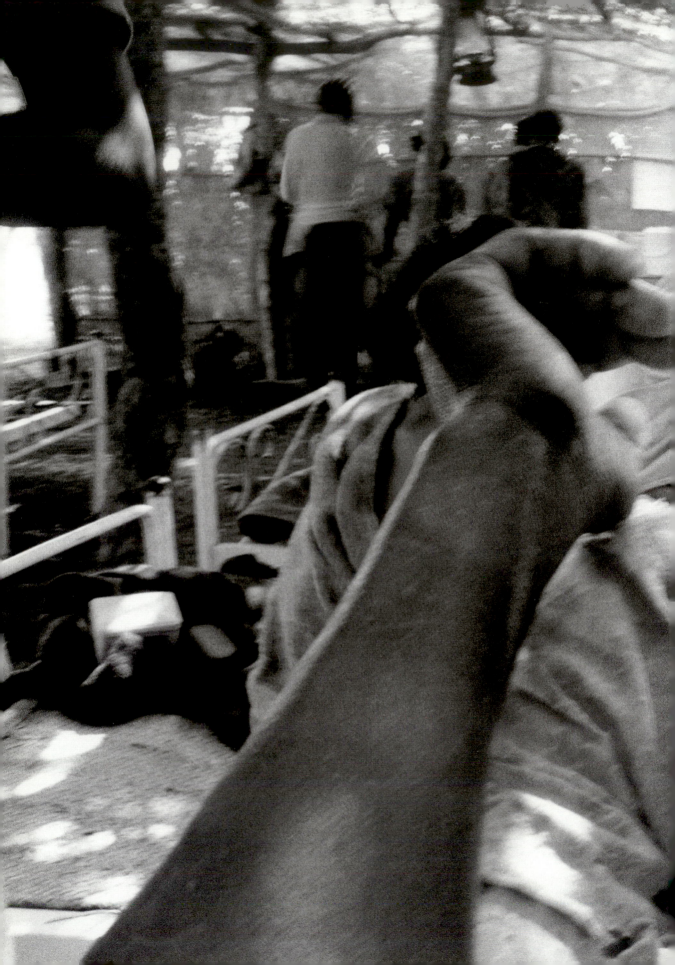

fourteen of us lived became a hostile place with people who didn't speak.

Somalia was less insane, but similar things happened. Some of our translators got arrested outside of the refugee camp on their day off. The team paid their fines. Then it happened again, and the fines were larger. Then it happened with one of the translator's family members, and when several of us questioned why we were paying there was a fight.

Thailand and Somalia were much easier places than Fau 3. In Thailand scores of doctors and nurses from all over the world lived in tiny Aranyapathet, an exotic border town. We had huge parties at night, dancing on a teak floor (rented from the local Buddhist monastery) under a parachute canopy hung from the trees. Amy's lonesome, and it's fine with me that she sees Nuur. But her social privileges are not an issue worth fighting about with Abdulmonim.

After letting off steam for a few more minutes, Amy announced that she was absolutely "a cinder." In expatriate slang, "burned out" is exceeded by "burnt to a crisp," which is exceeded by "burnt to a cinder." The next day Amy Greer left for Kassala to buy tribal gold. She was gone almost a week. She had been in camp four days since her previous break.

April 9

Today was the first day with no recorded deaths since Fau 3 opened. Before we could enjoy this good moment, we learned that three of the four water pumps were stolen last night.

We all suspect the Sudanese contractor Hadibai, the man who has charged us three times the normal rate to mud up the walls of our *tukuls*. Hadibai is a man with a powerful presence and a very oily charm. He brings us ice as a present, and from the ice most of us have gotten Giardia (a form of diarrhea). Siam, our guard, intensely distrusts him. Several times they've screamed at each other, because whenever Hadibai comes here Siam trails him like a watchdog, suspicious that he may steal from us.

Until we can set up the spare pump, REST has organized a bucket brigade of children to fill the water tanks.

April 10

Food distribution today, and I spoke to the CARE supervisor, a Ph.D. graduate student here for six months' field work. He's just come from Wad Kowli, where CARE conducted a census because they suspected they were delivering too many rations. They revised the population figure down from seventy thousand to forty-five thousand.

"So what," was the response of the official from the United States Agency for International Development (USAID), supplier of the grain. The CARE supervisor was astonished at the indifference to this mammoth overcount. On the surface it didn't make sense. The people in this camp have not been receiving enough food, and we've been told all along that there is a shortage. Just a few weeks ago, we were told that the ration for Fau 3 was to be cut.

Then the CARE supervisor realized that the twenty-five thousand extra rations were apparently being funneled across the border in REST trucks to feed the TPLF (Tigre Peoples Liberation Forces). In the midst of this disaster, our government appears to be using the starving refugees as camouflage to supply a rebel army fighting a Communist regime.

It's not enough just to feed people because they are starving. Humanitarian aid always seems to be used for political ends or to hide military aid. Vice President Bush was in Sudan last month, visiting the refugee camps. The newspaper headlines were about starving refugees, and medicine, and food. I wonder how many pennies of medicine we get for every dollar of secret military aid?

April 11

The field shower has finally been erected, but the nozzle fitting was put in backward, and the shower does not work. The *tukuls* are being mudded up, and all our belongings are piled outside on the beds. Each day everything gets covered with a new layer of dust. Most of the thatch fence around the compound perimeter has been mudded to about two feet off the ground to keep snakes from wriggling through. Last night Candy saw a snake coming through the fence when she was in the latrine with her pants down and happened to shine her flashlight beam on the fence in front of her. Tom calls our compound the "two-toned snake pit," because the perimeter walls are now two shades of brown.

We've set up a laboratory, which consists of a microscope, a hand centrifuge, some glass slides, and material to stain specimens. It was initially unimaginable to use a lab for individual patients. We took out the microscope to confirm the meningitis epidemic. We also used it to test a patient for relapsing fever, because we heard the disease was present in Ethiopia and didn't know if it existed here. We've discovered that it does and now treat people accordingly.

Early on the lab was most useful to develop and test treatment guidelines. The French team at Wad Kowli, Médecins Sans Frontières, tested a large group of patients who complained of fever and shaking chills and found that most did have malaria. So patients with those complaints automatically get malaria pills and don't see a doctor. Now we are examining sputum samples from people we suspect have tuberculosis. We hope to make a list and soon start a treatment program.

I was in the lab when the midwives asked me to help with a woman in labor. I examined the woman and couldn't figure out which part of the baby was coming out of the birth canal first nor why the labor had failed to progress. Something was clearly wrong. The amniotic fluid was the color and consistency of pea soup, a serious warning sign. The mother needed a cesarean section, which is impossible in the camp, and there was no way to transport her to a regional hospital. I collected tubing and sterile solution to suction out the baby's lungs and stomach after the birth and instructed the midwives.

There was no progress all afternoon. That night I spoke to the nurse midwife from Fau 2, who remembered a similar patient when she worked in rural Yemen several years ago. She tried an operation to widen the woman's pelvis, but there was horrible bleeding, and the baby still did not survive. There is no choice but to wait for nature to take its course.

(When I got to the ward the next morning, I found a happy mother and a perfect, healthy baby.)

April 12

Another cool gorgeous night, but two strange dreams. In one my cousin had a strange scar on his forehead, which he said was from an operation. It had been the worst type of brain tumor. Then a neurologist friend from San Francisco was saying, "Even with only a microscopic-size tumor they die by four months. They all die." It had been a year.

In my other dream Wren, a doctor at Fau 2, had a nervous breakdown. He was exhausted to the point of collapse and simply could not work. We were all talking together. He was sitting there physically unable to get up. He said he was going to Belgium to open some quasi-medical clinic. The only things he still felt able to do were take blood pressure and pulse.

April 13

Halfway through clinic this morning, there was a case that made me realize I can't take much more. The patient was a beautiful 41-year-old woman. She was led over to me by her 5-year-old daughter because she can not see. The woman began

(page 114)
Fau 3 refugee camp, April 1985. Women praying.

having trouble with her sight at Tukulubab three months ago, and she tried several times to get help. I went over to the ward to get Donna's ophthalmoscope, and I examined her eyes. Glaucoma has left her totally blind. Three months ago her vision could have been saved. Now her optic nerve is destroyed, and she is permanently blind.

When I told her nothing could be done to restore her sight she cried. She has three other children—one still an infant—and her husband is not in this camp. I don't know how she has been managing, or how she will get herself and her children back to their home in Tigre.

After she was led out, I left the clinic. I told my workers I needed to take care of something and that I would be right back. I walked over to the feeding center and went into the storeroom. I found a hidden place behind some boxes, and I sat by myself on a sack of grain. I took a drink of water and stared at the wall.

Ten minutes later, when I got back to the clinic, the crowds and stretchers and flies and crying babies were still there.

April 14

Brian has gone to Khartoum for a break. This morning I walked around the inpatient ward with Candy, a nurse practitioner, who will run the hospital in Brian's place.

We reviewed the patients and discussed how she should manage. I told her that her task is basically simple: Every patient needs as much as possible to eat and drink, and for each patient, she should pick the most likely antibiotic. After two or three days, if the patient isn't getting better, she should switch antibiotics or add a second drug. If the patient looks about to die and she can't decide, she should *start* with two drugs.

It sounds crude, but this is the reality of medical care in

Fau 3. We can treat dehydration, malnutrition, and infectious disease. After clinic each day I will go to the hospital, and we will review any cases that are a problem.

April 15

The clinic no longer has the atmosphere of a food riot. Much of the reason is fewer patients, about a hundred and fifty each day instead of two or three hundred. There are also fewer devastating illnesses. It's been more than two weeks since the last case of meningitis. It's satisfying to see the clinic slowly acquiring some of the qualities of a medical facility.

There are now rules that we prescribe only one drug at a time and that patients must have their health card, so we can see what was already done. We were seeing the same people come back day after day. They took one pill, and if that didn't work they took all the rest. Or they decided that they wanted a shot because a friend had gotten one.

We consult together about difficult cases, and I spend a large part of my time teaching, endlessly repeating several basic themes: Always try the simplest things first. Always balance the possible advantages of treatment with the possible harm. Always look for common things that we can cure like malnutrition, vitamin deficiencies, infections, or anemia.

I promoted Araya to "examiner" and gave him my extra stethoscope. He's the only Tigrayan with medical skills. The others are Amharic, not part of the camp's famine refugees. There's tension between them and Araya. When the camp opened, the Amharic staff pointed out that Araya couldn't be an examiner as he claimed, because he speaks no English; and in Ethiopia, English skills are required before you can be an examiner. IRC went along with this, and his responsibilities were limited. He got around it by holding his own clinics late in the day and at night. I don't care about his official training.

I've worked with him, checked his cases, tested him. He has experience, a quick mind, and common sense. I suspect he got his medical experience on the battlefield with the TPLF.

Today he and I examined a child carried into the clinic by his mother for an injection. The child was emaciated almost to the point of death. No cough, no fever, just pencil-thin arms and legs, swollen belly, ribs sticking out like a skeleton. I examined the child, and on the medical card I wrote a familiar diagnosis: "Severe malnutrition—refer to Therapeutic Feeding."

Araya explained, but the child's mother could not accept that we offered only food when she could see that her child was approaching death. She insisted on an "injection," the favorite Western medicine. She argued and got angry. As her voice became louder, I could see desperation and fear in her face.

These confrontations are rude reminders of the cultural distance between us and the refugees. I often feel like I'm squinting through a pinhole and seeing a mirage. A language barrier keeps us from talking, and we are constantly under the pressure of time. We know so little about these people we are trying to help.

About the injection, I superficially understand. In Somalia and Uganda it was the same. The people valued injections much more than pills or anything else. Tribal or folk medicine often is given as a single dramatic painful treatment. Injections fit this model that they already know and believe.

I refused to give the injection, and when the woman carried her child out of the clinic she looked at me in a way that I would like to forget.

April 16

Donna is back, after three weeks in Khartoum and Gedaref convalescing from the snake bite. Her motivation in returning here escapes me. I can see how hard it is for her to get started again, and I wonder if personal demons or angels led her back to Fau 3.

After dark Donna and I went to meet Abdulmonim's family. They have just come to join him in his new house. When I first arrived he lived alone in a small compound fifty yards from ours. With a quiet sense of humor, he referred to the shabby white tent in which he then lived as "the White House." A flock of thin nervous chickens shared his compound. The chickens seemed to be constantly trying to scratch their way over the thatch fence and escape. They usually failed. But one evening I saw one of the roosters make it over the fence. I watched the rooster look at the endless horizon with not a tree or hint of shelter. Then I saw the bird walk around the compound, and go back in through the front gate.

Abdulmonim asked if we would give his 18-year-old daughter a job during her school vacation. He asked if she could work with children in the feeding center. He feels it's important for her to learn to help people less fortunate and to understand that charity is fundamental to Islam. Abdulmonim and I also talked about going fishing together in the canal.

Back at camp we were visited by reporters from the London *Times*, Voice of America, and the BBC. As we walked over to the hospital, I pointed to the meningitis ward, which is now empty. When we entered the hospital, I looked at the journalists. The shock or horror that I expected to see on their faces was not there. It made me pause. The ward seemed orderly. There were empty beds. None of the patients appeared on the verge of death. I suddenly felt very odd, as if there was nothing to tell. We've been so busy that we haven't seen the change. The crisis at Fau 3 is coming under control.

April 17

I sent a woman with cerebral malaria into the hospital two days ago. She was comatose with high fever and seizures, and

(page 120)
Fau 3 refugee camp, April 15, 1985. The sun shelter collapses on fifty people waiting in clinic.

at that time I thought her chance of survival was poor. On the ward today the woman looked even worse, and Donna was giving her intravenous quinine as well as the standard malaria treatment and high doses of penicillin for possible pneumonia. I asked Donna if she needed help and briefly looked around the ward. Things did not look bad. Donna said she was almost done, so, at 3:00 P.M., I left.

Now, at 7:00 P.M., Donna has just returned. As she was about to leave the hospital, the woman with cerebral malaria died. The woman's family was hysterical, so rather than leaving Donna made rounds again. She stayed four hours and saw every patient on the entire ward another time. I see this extra activity as an intensely personal drama that was acted out on a ward with patients, but it really involved Donna and no one else. Perhaps it was an attempt to gain some feeling of control over a reality that for all of us has been intractable and overwhelming.

April 18

I'll be leaving in two days. This morning, instead of examining children in the feeding centers, Donna headed over to the ward to organize a surprise farewell party for me. On the way she met Jessica, who told her to forget the idea. Jessica understands my feelings and knows that a party is not something I would want or enjoy. Donna continued on to the ward. Shortly after she got there she was stung by a scorpion. A nurse ran to the clinic to get me, and when I got to the ward Donna was lying in one of the beds next to a refugee, tearful and in a great deal of pain. I injected her foot with anesthetic, and I was confused about what she was doing there.

In two days, when it's time for me to leave, I wish I could vanish instantaneously. I've never been good at leave taking or endings, nor comfortable with parties on my behalf, nor with public thanks. And this time, because I can't bear to stay any longer at Fau 3, I feel that I've failed.

These refugee camps breed such intense intimacy among the expatriates and with the refugee workers. We've left the usual content of our lives five thousand miles behind; and the content of their lives, the troubles and problems, become our common ground. We work long hours side by side, and as friendships develop the workers look to us with limitless needs. We are constantly approached for jobs for friends, clothes, pens, salary increase, sponsorship for immigration to the United States. These are legitimate needs, but they have nothing to do with why we were sent here. So much of it tugs at deep emotions inside me, and it's unwelcome. These relationships have desertion built in, as well as much else that is unfair.

Tonight after dinner Siam called me to the gate. I walked over and found seven of the translators and medical workers standing silently in the dark, behind the wooden poles. They looked very troubled, and they hesitated when I asked them what was wrong. Finally, after several awkward moments, they said they came to ask if it was true that I was going to leave Fau 3.

April 19

Last night Jessica woke me at 11:00 P.M. to come help Donna, who was hysterical that a bug had crawled into her ear. I looked in her ear and washed it out but never found a bug. Finally Donna settled down and went back to sleep. I went back to sleep and dreamed about pizza and cold beer.

Abdulmonim came into the clinic this morning to have me check his blood pressure, and we made plans to go fishing this afternoon at 5:00 P.M. He also told me a fantastic story about some Japanese people looking for witnesses of an unidentified flying object, a UFO. The land rover I saw drive through camp yesterday evidently didn't carry journalists, relief workers, politicians, or government officials. It was a delegation from the Cherry Blossom Project, sent here from Japan.

About three months ago a missionary priest working in Tigre reported in a letter that some of the peasants in his province had seen something unusual in the sky on Christmas Eve. This information reached the Cherry Blossom Project, a foundation in Japan devoted to study of UFOs. They dispatched investigators to Ethiopia. When the investigators got there, they discovered that the witnesses were gone. The people from that particular village were dead from the famine, sent to the south, or had become refugees in Sudan. So the Cherry Blossom Project dispatched a team to Sudan. They have already been to several other refugee camps looking for eyewitness accounts of this possible sighting of a UFO.

5:00 P.M.

Abdulmonim just sent his son over to cancel the fishing trip and also to bring the Cherry Blossom Project brochure. It's a glossy color magazine about UFOs, including beautiful pictures of famous skylines from around the entire world, with arrows pointing to tiny specks or little clouds in the sky that are supposed to be UFOs.

April 20

At 3:00 P.M. today I drove out of Fau 3. I felt defeated, relieved, and totally spent. The final process of leaving was painful, and Eiosis cried. I hadn't told her, or Siam, because I just couldn't deal with more sadness. About two hours before I left I went to get my clothes, and she gestured that tomorrow they would be hung to dry. I explained that I needed them today, that I would leave today. Then came the tears. I was also very upset, and I couldn't think of anything to say and said things that were ridiculous. I told her perhaps we would open a restaurant together in San Francisco, a restaurant specializing in lentils, and I told her that I knew I would always have a second mother in Tigre, and, mercifully, the translator then got called away and it was not possible to say anything more.

Just after our car pulled out, a terrible twister, a "dust devil," came right through the IRC compound at Fau 3. It went through the latrine and spilled an open case of toilet paper high into the air. Several rolls of pink toilet paper un-raveled and flew about. Jessica later said she was certain that this was meant as a ticker-tape farewell for me from the spirits of Fau 3.

(page 126)
Leaving Fau 3, April 20, 1985. At 3:00 P.M. today, feeling defeated, relieved, and totally spent, I drove out of Fau 3.

THE RESPITE

Vacation in Gedaref, Kassala, Suakin, and Port Sudan, April 22–April 29, 1985

(opposite)
Port Sudan, April 1985.
Camels wander the streets
like stray dogs and eat out
of the garbage dumpsters.

(page 130)
Gedaref, April 22, 1985. My
first night away from Fau 3
I'm unable to sleep, and at
5:00 A.M., with the first
light, I'm wandering the
streets with my camera.

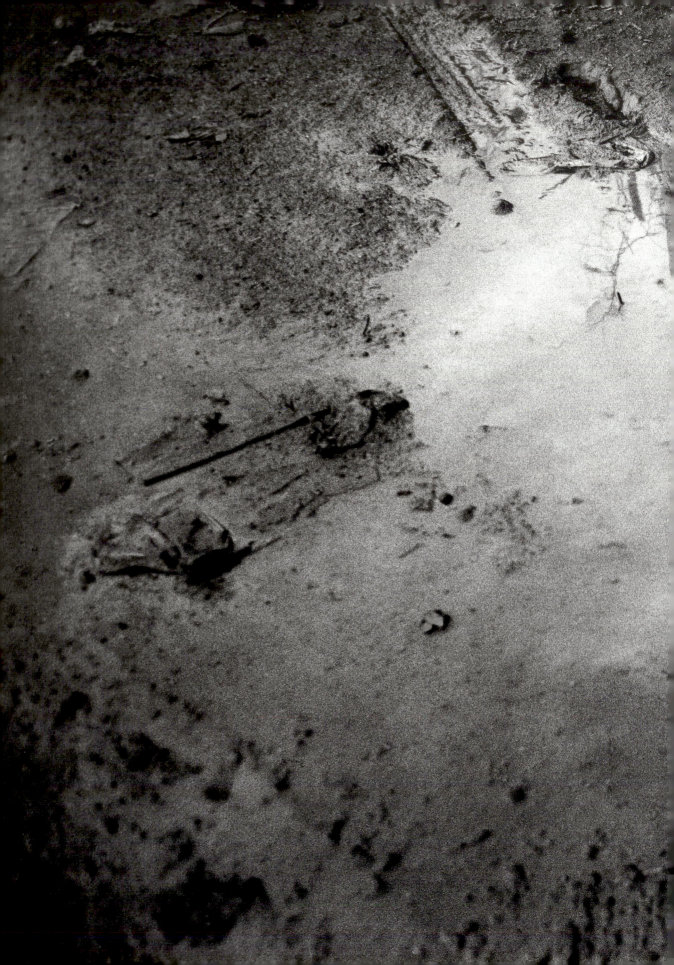

April 22

I now sit in the IRC guest house in Gedaref. The place is a dusty mess. No water. No electricity. Bunches of assorted foreign and American kids drifting in and out and lounging around. Small groups of relief workers stopping in on their way to or from different camps. The outbound ones all look eager, the incoming workers all look thin and tired. A German couple living here has just adopted a Sudanese infant, because, they tell me, the father has left home and the Sudanese mother is too young to take care of it. The German woman looks about 18.

A nutritionist going to Fau 3 arrived last night. She explained how we should have immediately set up a solar cooker and fed the children differently. This morning the nutritionist visited the market for shopping and lunch, and now she is sitting on the bathroom floor throwing up. It's a suitable prelude for Fau 3.

I ache whenever I think of Fau 3, and I know that I can not return there. Tim White, the program director for IRC, asked me if they should make plane reservations for me to leave Sudan early. I said no, that after my vacation I want to work. But I don't know what I'll do.

I was supposed to meet Martha here yesterday. We planned to catch the weekly UNHCR plane from Gedaref to Kassala (five hours by bus or thirty minutes by plane) and then get a bus to Port Sudan for a week by the Red Sea. So far no Martha, and it is impossible to get word to or from Wad Kowli. The plane leaves this morning in an hour. It looks like we'll miss it.

April 23

Martha arrived late last night. She just finished vaccinating for meningitis at Wad Kowli, and that was the reason for the delay—forty-two thousand people in a single week, and

Martha organized and managed the whole show. She says it went great. I last saw Martha three months ago just before she left San Francisco. She's lost at least twenty pounds since then and paces around chain smoking, bursting with nervous energy. What a pleasure to be with an old friend.

I got up by myself at 5:00 A.M. and wandered around Gedaref. I walked through the markets and watched the butchers preparing goat and beef. Because of the famine, meat in Gedaref is cheap and plentiful. There's no grain to feed the animals. Rather than wait for them to starve, the animals are slaughtered for whatever price that can be obtained. I sat on the ground with several men wearing turbans and enjoyed a cup of *jabenai*, strong ginger-flavored coffee served in tiny chipped white-enamel cups. I bought some bread, and before 8:00 A.M. I was back at the IRC guest house.

Martha and I caught the 2:00 P.M. bus to Kassala and arrived at dusk. We looked in the gold and tribal jewelry shops, ate grilled chunks of liver and beans and tomatoes with our hands in a sidewalk restaurant, and then went to bed. We have to be at the bus at 5:30 in the morning to fight for a seat on the 6:00 A.M. departure for Port Sudan.

Even from this brief glimpse, Kassala seems exotic and interesting. I'm told that it's the traditional crossing point between eastern Sudan and Ethiopia, a crossroads for all the tribes in this region. Hadendowa men stroll the streets with turbans carrying long tribal swords. Rashaida women walk about wearing black veils, with rings of heavy silver jewelry from their necks, ankles, wrists, ears, and noses. There are people from the Beni-Amir tribe with three scars on each cheek. Boys herd goats through sandy unpaved streets, and camel riders weave between the cars. Several miles from the town massive rock buttes rise dramatically from the flat desert landscape, warning of the brutal mountains of nearby Ethiopia. They look like ghostly clouds when we drove in at dusk.

One of those rock buttes out near the border is named

(page 134)
Gedaref, April 23, 1985.
Waiting for the bus to leave
for Kassala.

Tukulubab. The camp that first housed the refugees of Fau 3 was in the shadow of that rock. I am told that Tukulubab is now completely deserted. I have an urge to visit the place, but there's no way to get there and no time.

April 24

Martha and I sit eating ice cream in the lobby at the Red Sea Hotel, a wonderful dilapidated British colonial relic of the past. Poor Martha—I talked nonstop the entire nine-hour bus trip from Kassala. Out poured all the bitterness, pain, anger, and frustration of the last two months, far more than I dreamed was inside me, and Martha listened sympathetically.

She had her own stories from Wad Kowli. She arrived there in the midst of a measles epidemic, and, best they could count, twelve hundred children were lost to measles in the single month of January. Martha said that cultural notions probably contributed to the high mortality. Refugees often didn't bring in children sick with measles for medical care. Perhaps because of the rash or the sensitivity of the eyes to light, the refugees thought measles was caused by evil spirits. Maybe they regarded it as punishment for abandoning their farms in Tigre. When Martha went through the camp looking for children with measles, she would go to huts where she heard a clanging noise. Inside she would find an older child banging on a pot to scare away the evil spirits, with a younger child wrapped up in the darkest corner of the hut, sick with measles. Martha worked nonstop the first three weeks, then got sick with exhaustion and dysentery and was taken to Gedaref, where she slept three days. On her first night back, she was bitten by a scorpion, and she sat up all night in agony with ice on her finger.

She said in the first few months a continuous stream of journalists came through Wad Kowli, and workers often felt like they were expected to be guides and entertain the journalists. She described to me how she started to say her first word of an interview for NBC Nightly News and a fly flew into her mouth.

April 25

Port Sudan is in one of those eddies that spin off from the currents of time. It appears as if nothing new has been built, and nothing painted or repaired, since the mid-1950s.

Near the front desk of the Red Sea Hotel, there is a beautiful wooden plaque listing record fish caught in the Red Sea by hotel guests. All the names sound like British diplomats or soldiers, and this was probably a main stop on the way to India, Rangoon, and Singapore in the great days of the British Empire. The last entry on the wooden plaque is for a Colonel Crawford who caught a twenty-six-pound barracuda in 1939.

The rooms and lobby all have high ceilings and overhead fans. The huge stuffed chairs in the lobby seem waiting for Humphrey Bogart or Sidney Greenstreet. In front of the hotel is a sandy open space, once a grand colonial garden, and next door is the administrative building, with old cannons and a similar empty space in front. Camels roam the streets like stray dogs, eating out of the garbage dumpsters.

Three blocks away we bought fabric from an elderly Lebanese man who moved here in 1942. He told us we should go for a tour of the harbor in the glass-bottom boat from the Red Sea Hotel. Back at the hotel no one had ever heard of such a thing, and later we learned that he had taken his boat ride on his last visit to the hotel, in 1956.

April 26

We've met a number of relief people who are working in areas other than medicine. A group of us had dinner at an outside restaurant next to the water, and we talked into the night, trying to fit the pieces together.

This seaport is the first in a series of bottlenecks. The

(page 138)
Suakin, April 28, 1985.

docks are antiquated and can't handle the volume of supplies. Boats filled with food wait outside the harbor. They don't have enough trained people or equipment to handle the unloading, and then they don't have warehouse space in which to put the supplies, or a system to keep track of things.

When supplies are finally ready to be moved out of Port Sudan, there aren't enough trucks. There is not enough fuel. There aren't phones to coordinate the transports. The old and chronically overloaded trucks break down. Then they simply sit by the side of the road, like another dead animal, because there's a shortage of spare parts, mechanics, and repair shops. The single road out of Port Sudan toward the camps is unsafe to drive at night. Camels and donkeys like to sleep on the road because the asphalt keeps them warm during the cold desert nights.

Coping with this disaster is like trying to put out a five-alarm fire with an old garden hose that has rusted attachments and is full of leaks. In the camps we hold the empty hose and grind our teeth in frustration.

April 27

A few days at Arous, a "European" resort an hour north of Port Sudan. It closed a few weeks ago when all the European staff fled the country during the coup. It just reopened with local staff. We were the only guests. There was beautiful snorkeling along the reef immediately in front of the hotel. Camels lying on the beach lifted their heads and stared as we went in the water.

Martha and I got up at dawn and hiked to a nearby lagoon to see birds: lesser flamingos, spoonbills, storks, ospreys, and several types of egret and heron. We ended up plodding through deep mud to get a good view, but we didn't care.

April 28

A picnic at the ghost town of Suakin. In the days before the British, Suakin was the most powerful city on the Red Sea. It controlled the trade in pearls and slaves. Rudyard Kipling wrote a poem about how "the Fuzzy Wuzzys cut up our troops in front of Suakin." When the British took control, they needed to deepen the harbor to accommodate their larger ships. The Suakin city leaders refused. So the British deepened the harbor sixty kilometers to the north, connecting Port Sudan to the railroad and bypassing Suakin. The slave trade was suppressed. And the Japanese later captured the pearl market by discovering how to culture pearls. Commerce went elsewhere, and Suakin died.

Back at the hotel over dinner, we laughed about how we had lost touch with civilization, particularly about food. When we sat down the group at the next table had just gotten up. Without hesitating, I got up and went over to see what they had leftover. With delight and no sense of embarrassment, I returned to our table with bread, a few french fries, and a piece of chicken.

April 29

Now back at the IRC guest house in Gedaref. I feel much better, gained a few pounds, and slept several nights without bad dreams. A college girl from England gave me a haircut. I went to the market by myself for dinner, and as I wandered around afterward, a man tried to sell me a monkey. The price was very cheap. For a moment I thought of buying it and setting it loose to scamper around in the IRC guest house.

I spoke with Tim White, the IRC director. Brian Cole has given notice that he is leaving, because he "doesn't want to provide care for guerilla fighters"—the TPLF—and he is convinced that half the camp is TPLF. This is nonsense, but I sympathize with his urge to leave Fau 3.

I'm still in limbo. Martha already left for Wad Kowli, and I've arranged to go out there tomorrow. Martha says she'll find work for me, which would be great, but it is unclear how long I will stay or what I will do.

(page 144)
Eastern Sudan, April 29, 1985. Driving through a sandstorm on the way back from vacation.

DEPARTURES AND DISLOCATIONS
Wad Kowli Refugee Camp
and Khartoum,
April 30–May 24, 1985

(opposite)
Wad Kowli refugee camp,
May 1985.

(page 148)
Wad Kowli refugee camp,
May 1985.

April 30

As we drove to Wad Kowli, the flat landscape gradually gave way to hills and broken terrain cut by *wadis* (dry stream beds) deep as the landrover. Leafless thorn trees became increasingly common. We passed several great baobab trees looking like roots stuck upside down in the earth. The mountains of Ethiopia gradually became visible in the distance, and after three hours of bumping over the rutted dirt track, we entered camp.

Wad Kowli is a chaotic sprawl of thatch huts among the trees that line the far bank of the Atbara River. The reported population is now forty thousand. How different it looks from the orderly rows of ragged tents in the middle of emptiness that is Fau 3.

The Atbara River is the last tributary of the Nile. This branch is now dry, but the rocky 100-yard-wide riverbed is an impressive sight. Tall forking palm trees dominate the horizon. I've already seen numerous birds, including a stunning turquoise Abyssinian roller. There are monkeys and camels. This is the Africa that I love, and it's a relief to my eye and spirit after the desolation of Fau 3.

The IRC compound is huge, with twelve well-made *tukuls*, two excellent showers, and a large dining/meeting area. There are two other medical relief groups working at Wad Kowli with compounds next door. The French group, Médecins Sans Frontières, runs the adult clinics and hospital; and the British group, Save the Children Fund (SCF), runs pediatric care. It feels like a congenial, enthusiastic community. Since the camp is the doorway between Ethiopia and Sudan, there's a palpable excitement in the air.

May 1

I've been asked to fill in as the camp's medical coordinator. I will run meetings, track vital statistics, report activities, and handle any new problems.

IRC runs public health and supervises mass movement of refugees in and out of camp. Three hundred people came in across the border from Ethiopia last night. They were held overnight in a large shelter at the edge of camp.

This morning I helped process the new arrivals. When we got to the *recuba* (shelter), they were sitting in absolute silence as people from COR (Commissioner of Refugees) and REST walked among them, counting out loud in Tigrinyan and Arabic. The people must wait until the counts absolutely agree. Martha says it was uncanny how silent even a crowd ten times as large could be. After the counts matched, everyone received meningitis vaccine and capsules of vitamin A. Children under 12 also received measles vaccine and were screened for malnutrition. Those that are undernourished got wrist bracelets, admitting them to the feeding centers. Finally, the refugees were assigned ration cards and places in camp.

Several hundred new arrivals every few days is only a trickle. Martha says there were periods in February and March when two or three thousand people arrived each day, and we fear that mass arrivals could begin again without warning. The best guess is that there are still twenty thousand people on their way here: "in the pipeline to Sudan," is what people say. We've heard a separate rumor that a camp in Ethiopia's Gondar Province, housing fifty to sixty thousand people from Tigre, was just burned down by the Ethiopian army and the people ordered back to their villages. There's no food in their villages, and twenty thousand of those people are expected at Wad Kowli as well.

(page 152)
Hospital, Wad Kowli
refugee camp, May 1985.

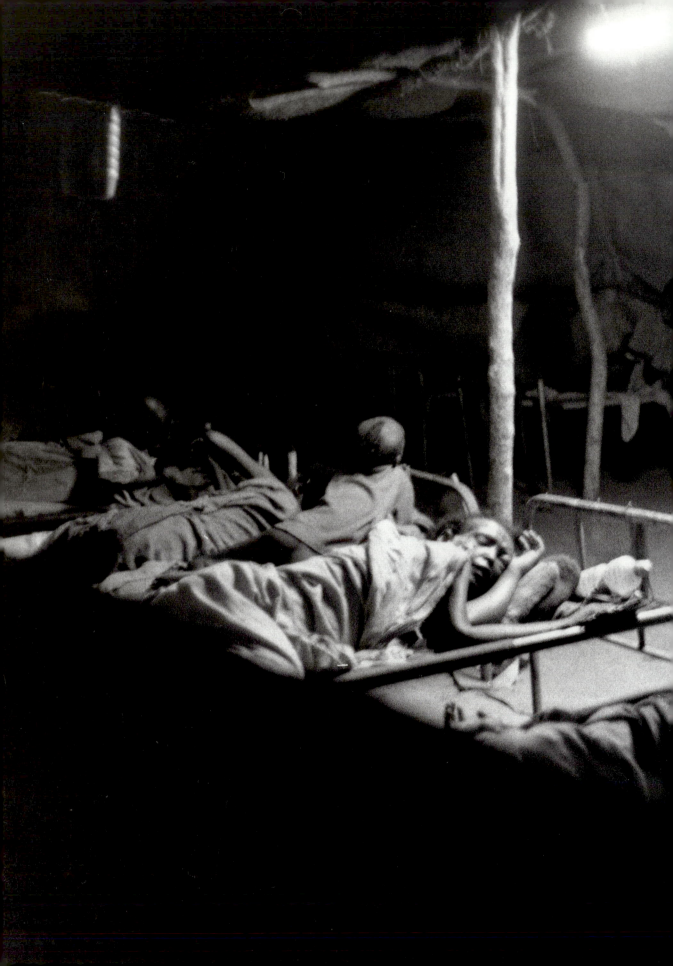

May 2

In February the Sudanese announced: "In two weeks Wad Kowli will close."

First it was a problem with finding water for ninety thousand people from a river that had run dry. In March to April about half the people in Wad Kowli were moved to a new camp at Sefawa, forty miles away. There was only one death in transit and only one miscalculation. The last group of refugees that were moved to Sefawa was sent before there was shelter for them. The refugees arrived late in the day, and during the night they dismantled the thatch walls and roof of a huge, empty feeding center to get building material. The expatriate workers woke up the next morning and were astonished to find that the new feeding center had vanished.

Since that first evacuation there's been a series of precarious temporary solutions to the water problem. There are some pools in the riverbed still holding water. Water is now pumped from a pool thirty minutes from camp and trucked here, but both the trucks and pumps are unreliable. As usual we lack spare parts and are chronically short of fuel.

In a month we will be in the rainy season, and the water problem will solve itself. But we'll have a new problem. The paved road ends at Gedaref, and the dirt track that runs here will be impassable, cut by *wadis* full of water, and intractable mud. Wad Kowli will be cut off and impossible to supply. Villages in this region are tiny, because that's all the environment will support. Like a patient on a respirator in an intensive care unit, Wad Kowli's survival depends on continuous external support.

So the second major effort to empty this camp has just begun. We are sending people to a new camp being set up near the reservoir at Khasmr El Ghirba. On the way back from Port Sudan, Martha and I stopped there. At eight in the morning we saw the first group arrive. After traveling all night by truck from Wad Kowli, they looked shaken and exhausted. But no one had died.

We've learned from the disastrous evacuation of Tukulubab to the Fau camps. Now only open trucks are used with a limit of forty-five people in each one. In the move from Tukulubab to the Faus, closed trucks were packed with up to seventy people. We are careful to keep families and villages together, and a leader is assigned in each truck with a list of passengers. There is water in each truck, and a midpoint rest stop.

May 3

At sunrise Martha and I took a long photo walk up the river-bed, and we watched refugees washing clothes and fishing in the remaining stagnant ponds. Then we began work.

Shortly before 8:00 A.M. I went over to Osman Mekki's landrover to contact Ghirba about last night's evacuation. Osman Mekki is the project manager for Wad Kowli, and the short-wave radio for Wad Kowli is in his car. It took less than ten minutes to contact Ghirba, and I spoke to Simon, an Australian nurse who worked with me briefly at Fau 3. We reviewed the trip. There were no problems on the road or at Ghirba, and they are ready for more refugees.

The short-wave slang and place labels sound exotic and romantic as they crackle over the air: "Whiskey Kilo" for Wad Kowli, "Sierra Foxtrot" for Sefawa, and "Gulf Lima" for Ghirba Lake. Osman prefers "Mobile One" for Wad Kowli— more dignity—and at the radio he has great style and a low voice full of authority and control.

One of my other jobs is to chair the weekly meeting of the village elders. Today the elders made impassioned speeches asking for more food, more blankets, more clothing. I listened, took notes, and assured them I will try my best to help, and the meeting ended with a warm round of applause. I am told that

(page 156)
Evacuation center, Wad Kowli refugee camp, May 4, 1985. We are loading the refugees on trucks and moving them to another camp before the rainy season hits and we will be cut off from the outside.

(pages 157 and 158)
Wad Kowli refugee camp, May 6, 1985. Loading trucks for evacuation.

(page 160)
Wad Kowli refugee camp, May 6, 1985. Truck filled with refugees leaving on the all-night journey to Ghirba.

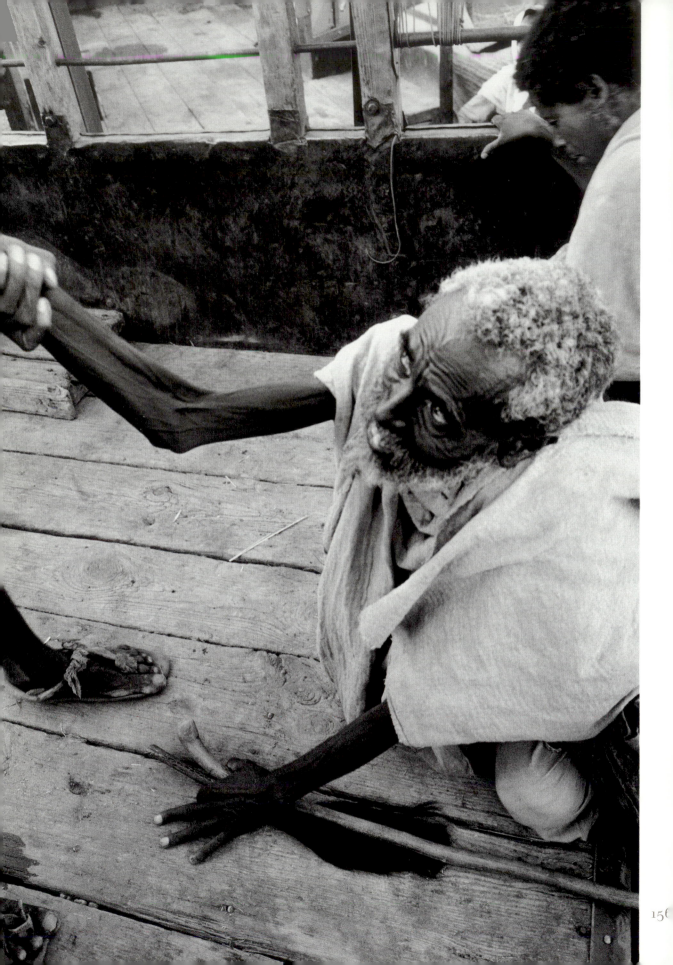

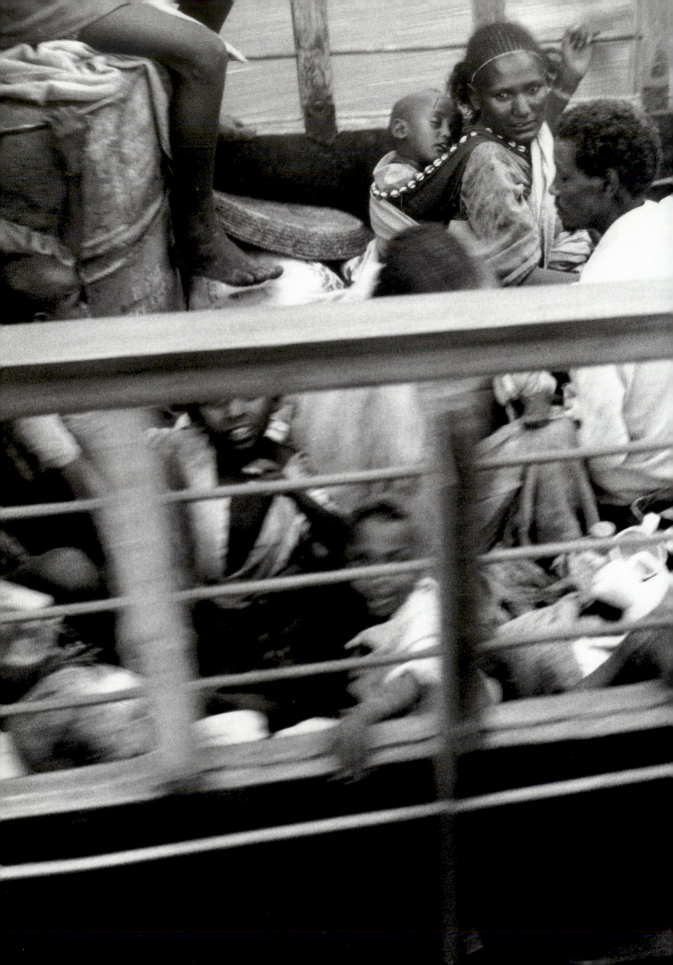

the topics of discussion at these meetings are almost always the same. In fact, there are no more blankets, clothing, or food to distribute.

May 4

The evacuation center echoes Ellis Island and countless other refugee stories of the last century. Crowds of people are waiting with all their belongings tied up in bundles. They shepherd their infants and children as they board crowded trucks headed to a strange place and an unknown future.

I spent the afternoon examining sick people scheduled for evacuation. While filling out the health cards, I spelled a village name five different ways before I realized the people were all from the same village: Jijka, Geyshka, Geechka, Gigika, Chichika. It's a classic story: someone totally illiterate in a language, transcribing names and sounds that don't exist in the recorder's own tongue. Again I thought back to Ellis Island and some well-meaning Irish clerk giving different people in the same Jewish family the names Cohn, Cohen, Kohn, Kahn, Conn . . .

May 5

With today's 8:00 A.M. radio message, I could feel the tension and worry in Simon's voice: "Stop evacuation. There is no water. I repeat, stop evacuation. There is no water."

Osman Mekki had heard that there were some difficulties setting up water for the new arrivals at Ghirba, but he assumed it was not a major problem. He told us that sixty trucks are on the way to Wad Kowli. The trucks must be used today, because tomorrow they must be at Wad Sherrife, near Kassala. Osman said we should try to get Ghirba back by radio. He made it clear that he is under great pressure to follow orders and reminded us we are running out of days before the rains, when we will be forced to stop evacuation. We are already dangerously behind schedule.

It was impossible to reach Ghirba again. At 2:00 P.M. sixty trucks arrived. One of the truck drivers had a written message for Osman Mekki from COR headquarters in Showak that confirmed refugees were to be moved today. We don't know if COR headquarters in Showak is aware of the water situation inside the Ghirba refugee camp. Best we understand from Simon's radio message this morning, if we send twenty-five hundred more people to Ghirba, they will have no water.

All afternoon we had meetings. After a long standoff, we wrote a memo to Osman Mekki claiming it was a medical necessity to defer evacuation, and acknowledging responsibility for the decision. Then we refused to load the trucks. We think we did the right thing, but it's impossible to know. We realize that Osman could have forced a move, and that delaying might risk his job.

And tonight something strange happened, as if we were being given notice that we must act with supreme care. At 9:00 P.M. someone noticed that a rim of the full moon had disappeared. Gradually, we witnessed a total eclipse. The lunar sky went black, and the stars became bright. We put out all the lights and sat in the middle of our compound watching the sky. Several shooting stars appeared near the shadowed moon. Across the river the camp came alive, and we could hear chanting and wails. To the Tigrayans a lunar eclipse is ominous, a sign of warning and dread.

May 6

A few days ago I asked Osman Mekki if I could go out to the border seven kilometers past camp. I'm curious about the place, and I think it's important to take a few pictures of

(page 164)
Ghirba refugee camp, May 1985. A child from Wad Kowli arrives at Ghirba holding his health card.

(page 166)
Wad Kowli evacuation center, May 1985. A mother and child too sick to travel to Ghirba are separated from their family and village and left behind.

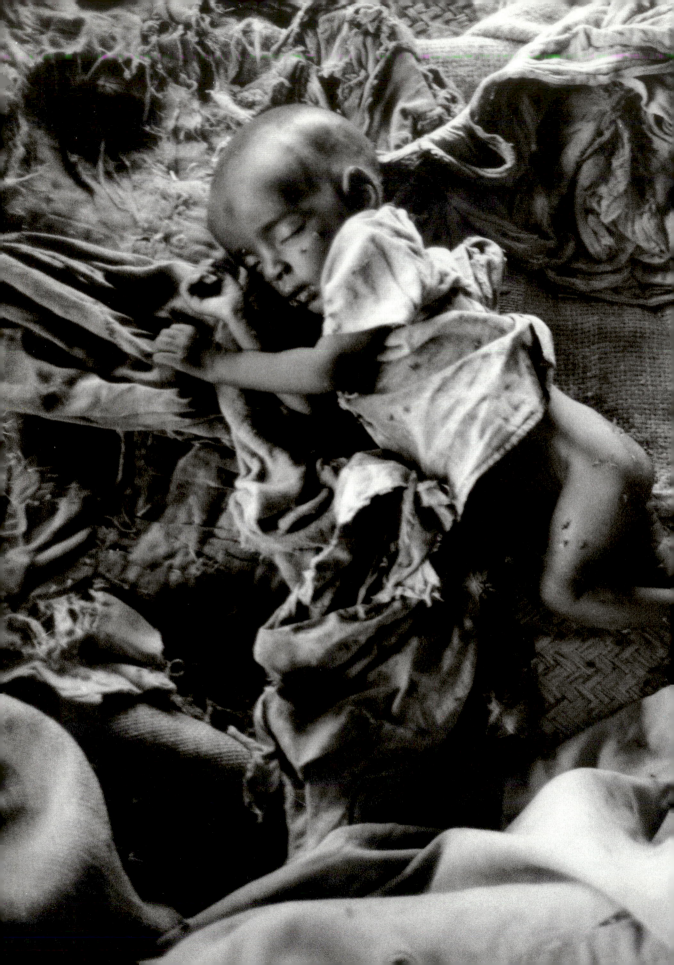

the actual border. He was polite but evasive and would only say, "the border is a very sensitive area," which apparently meant no.

This afternoon ten huge new Mercedes trucks passed through camp loaded with drums of diesel fuel that were covered with huge tarps. Actually, anything could have been under the tarps. This was the largest and most modern transport of any nature that I've witnessed since I've been in Sudan.

The only land route into Tigre goes through Wad Kowli. My translator says the trucks belong to the TPLF and that they are headed for the war. He also says that there is a TPLF military encampment on this side of the border, actually in the Sudan. This is what we read about in newspapers all the time, military spending versus programs for human welfare. I wish the newspaper stories could convey the rage I feel watching expensive modern materials go to an army, while in this camp we still lack cheap vitamin pills and other medicines to cure children with illnesses from the Middle Ages. I wonder if the money for those Mercedes trucks came from the United States, from emergency allocations labeled "humanitarian aid."

May 7

Today I heard about Sally Ann Coolidge's donkey project. It seems that about 750 donkeys arrived with the first wave of people coming out of Tigre. Several months later the donkey owners were transported on to Sefawa, forty miles farther inside Sudan, and they left their donkeys behind. It soon became apparent that there was a "donkey plague" in Wad Kowli. Donkey dung littered the camp. Donkeys ate the straw walls of the feeding center, and they brayed and copulated in the pediatric clinic. At a camp meeting the donkeys were formally identified as a "public health menace." Sally Ann Coolidge, the camp sanitarian, was put in charge of "donkey control."

Sally Ann is an uncomplaining woman with good judgment and excellent practical skills. But she can't resist giving unsolicited "helpful suggestions," and she loves to tune in the radio to Christian evangelical programs that no one else on the team can bear.

The donkey problem became a running thread through daily conversations. Sally Ann spent weeks on the problem and never lost her good humor. All the donkeys with owners at Sefawa were separated out. She identified the village of origin for each donkey, dyed pieces of rope different colors to make donkey necklaces for village identification, and hired little kids as herders. Finally, one triumphant day, a line of 750 donkeys left camp. Martha, then visiting Sefawa, described the fantastic sight of this donkey caravan marching into Sefawa shortly after sunrise. Everyone at Wad Kowli breathed a sigh of relief and congratulated Sally Ann.

But it turned out that Sefawa didn't want the donkeys either. A few days later the entire bizarre caravan marched back into Wad Kowli.

May 8

Again my day starts with an agitated message over the short-wave radio. Will Day, the SCF team leader at Sefawa refugee camp, says that two thousand people left camp last night on foot, headed in this direction. Without obvious plans or warning, the refugees packed up and set out for home. The departing refugees claimed that they have seeds buried at home, that the rains are coming, and they need to plant their seeds or they will have to stay another year. "We don't like it here," they said. "Our children die here."

Both SCF and REST tried to convince them not to leave. Many of the children wore feeding center arm bracelets, and when the mothers saw Will checking, they tore the bracelets off. Some of the SCF nutritionists and nurses who nurtured these children were in tears. They fear that many are too weak

(page 170)
Eastern Sudan, May 8, 1985. Refugees spontaneously began heading for Wad Kowli, the Ethiopian border, then home to Tigre.

(page 172)
Outskirts of Wad Kowli, daybreak, May 9, 1985. A refugee who had walked all night toward home.

to survive a three-week trip over rugged mountains, constantly sleeping outside and exposed.

The head of REST was very candid. REST cannot feed the people that are inside Tigre right now, he said. First REST told the people there was no water in the rivers—and when this didn't work, they tried telling them that the rivers were already too high to cross.

5:30 P.M.

Just back from a drive up the road to Sefawa with the UNHCR representative. We left at 2:00 P.M., and halfway to Sefawa we encountered a broken line of humanity, stretching over miles, hundreds of people walking on foot in the scorching sun. All their possessions, infants, and children too sick to walk, were carried on their backs or on their shoulders. The women wore their cooking pots on their heads like hats. It's forty miles from Sefawa to Wad Kowli, forty dry dusty miles in 120-degree heat. We decided to fill the landrover for the ride back.

Whenever we stopped the car got mobbed. The men forced their way to the front and started to pile their bundles in the back of the land rover or force bundles through the windows. Men tried to climb on the hood of the car, on the roof, or to hang on to the back of the car, standing on the fenders. I pushed and screamed in a language that none of them understood. After several episodes the landrover was packed with only women and children, and we returned to Wad Kowli. Somehow we stuffed seventeen people in that vehicle for the ride back, and it was so crowded that I feared an infant might get crushed when the car bumped and people flew into one another and against the sides. We made another trip before dark and radioed for trucks, but that will have to be arranged by the Sudanese.

May 9

I was up before sunrise and could hear sounds of people walking. Refugees from Sefawa streamed past our compound. They are walking across eastern Sudan, toward the mountains, back to their homes. I felt like I was watching a tide of history, receding, completing a cycle, carrying these people back from where they came. I stared in amazement. It was still before dawn. In the haunted gray light, it seemed like a dream.

At lunch we talked about why the refugees suddenly decided to go home. It's a mystery to us, and we wonder if there's any connection with the eclipse of the full moon that happened a few days ago.

One of the UNHCR officials told us about a young woman from Tigre who worked for him. Months ago, as the woman left her farm in Tigre, she had stopped and picked up five pebbles off her land. He saw her take the pebbles out, hold them, and weep.

The mood about repatriation was shattered abruptly when we saw smoke coming from a central area of the camp. For the fifth time since Wad Kowli opened, a cooking fire got out of control. With the extreme dryness, it was more like an explosion than a fire. When I arrived the flames were thirty feet high. We organized a bucket brigade and started a firebreak. The heat was terrible—it's 120 degrees this time of day without a fire.

Our efforts did nothing. We were afraid the fire would reach the treetops, where it would be impossible to control. Then the wind shifted and blew the fire into the empty riverbed, a natural firebreak. In about twenty minutes the fire was out, but an area one hundred yards long by fifty yards wide was scorched.

Three hundred families lost everything.

(page 176)
Wad Kowli refugee camp, May 9, 1985. For the fifth time since Wad Kowli opened, a cooking fire got out of control, destroying the homes of three hundred families before dying out in the empty riverbed.

(page 178)
Wad Kowli refugee camp, May 9, 1985. After the fire three women search in the ashes for any remaining possessions.

May 11

The migration back to Tigre has snowballed and turned into a huge, chaotic event. The Sudanese have organized trucks, and now people arrive each day from different camps, including the Faus, and Demizen, which is far to the south. Here at Wad Kowli we get no warning when the trucks will arrive nor of how many refugees are coming. Some days three thousand people arrive. With holdovers from the days before, as many as seven thousand people might be camping on the edge of Wad Kowli, and we have little time or resources for preparation. Shelter and water are big problems.

We've organized a medical program for those going back. We try to screen out those too sick to make the trip. I worked out simple guidelines of what to treat, and we have a crew packaging medicines to hand out. For prevention of scurvy we give a tablet of vitamin C to every person on departure, and this should be protective for up to two weeks. We give a capsule of vitamin A to every person to prevent blindness, and from counting how many capsules we give out comes the best numerical estimate on how many people depart each day. We try to identify health workers in each group, and we prepare instructions in Tigrinyan to go with health kits containing bandage, chloroquine, oral rehydration salts, and vitamin C. We give pregnant women a supply of iron/folate pills and birth kits containing a clean razor and string to cut and tie the umbilical cord.

Repatriation has caused a political storm in Khartoum. Yesterday three top officials arrived from UNHCR headquarters. They're here to see if this repatriation is truly voluntary or if the people are being coerced. The politics are complicated. Food from the stores at Wad Kowli is being released by Sudanese authorities to REST. REST is receiving several weeks ration (50 kilograms) for every person that returns. This has apparently been okayed by UNHCR and by CARE, the agency actually handling the food. But the American Embassy is against it, and UNHCR is being criticized. The United States is the major food donor and the major funding source for UNHCR.

May 12

At the meeting this morning we finished our planning paper for "001," Sudanese code for cholera. It's another of my tasks as medical coordinator. So far there have been no outbreaks in Sudan, but it's only a matter of time. As the doorway, Wad Kowli will be first. The BBC recently carried news about a major epidemic near Hargeysa in Somalia, and epidemics have been moving across Ethiopia. A French doctor from Médecins Sans Frontières told me about an epidemic at Korem camp, a place about the same size as Wad Kowli located in Wollo Province of Ethiopia. There were fourteen hundred cases with 30 percent mortality.

We do not mention cholera in the entire draft. The word is strictly forbidden, evidently carrying a stigma of national disgrace. "Acute gastroenteritis" and "001" are the acceptable terms. One of the Sudanese officials explained to me that if it is known that there is cholera in Sudan, "it will be bad for tourism."

May 13

An officer from the American Embassy was in camp today and ate lunch with us at the IRC compound. He evidently made the trip here from Khartoum because of the repatriation to Tigre. It was a peculiar visit, and it left me wondering.

The embassy official spent most of lunch lecturing to us. He said it's wrong for REST to receive food allocations for the people going back. First he suggested that REST was forcing the people to go back. Then he said the refugees were not healthy enough to go back and implied that it was our fault for

(page 182)
Wad Kowli refugee camp, May 1985. Refugees bathe, wash clothes, and get water from the stagnant ponds in the dry Atbara riverbed, source of our cholera epidemic.

(page 184)
Cholera ward, Wad Kowli refugee camp, May 15, 1985. A woman with cholera.

(page 185)
Cholera ward, Wad Kowli refugee camp, May 17, 1985. A child with cholera.

(page 186)
Wad Kowli refugee camp, May 17, 1985. Disinfecting the floor of the cholera ward.

letting them return. He told us the war in Tigre is now going against the TPLF and that the way back was blocked by ten thousand Ethiopian troops. He said there was still no food in Tigre and that the 50-kilogram ration for each person might permit them to get in, but not back out. Most of them will die, he said.

After eating lunch and giving his lecture, the embassy official was ready to return to Khartoum. He would not have laid eyes on the refugees that were repatriating if we had not insisted.

We drove to the departure site on the outskirts of Wad Kowli. No one from REST was there. We approached a group of men. I pointed to the distant hills and said "Tigre?" and they responded with enthusiasm. It was obvious they were generally healthy and that morale was extremely high. Nothing remotely suggested that they were being coerced.

I doubt if he understands how devastating their experience in Sudan has been and how desperately they want to go home. Maybe this repatriation will turn out badly. I don't see how anyone can know. Certainly there are frightening risks, but I suspect the information they possess through word of mouth is as accurate as any of our "intelligence." These people can make their own decisions.

May 14

I was walking out to monitor this evening's departure for Tigre when I saw a young woman with an infant tied to her back, sobbing hysterically. She was walking back in to camp all alone. She was at the transit point among those going home, and for some reason, at the last moment she did not leave. As I walked on I found myself wondering what could have happened. Did her husband order her back? Did she get separated? Did her village leave without her? Did she get last-minute word from the border that her village in Tigre was cut off by the fighting, or destroyed, or that there was no one left to go back to?

It's impossible for me to absorb this immense disaster. Every day I witness events that seem to bounce off without waking any feeling. Then a single element separates out. For an instant, I clearly see a single person and the tragedy strikes home.

I told Martha about the woman I saw crying. Martha had been farther down the road and was fuming about "those stupid boneheads" from a prominent American relief group now visiting Wad Kowli. It's a relief group that runs heart-wrenching, inaccurate advertisements in many magazines. Martha's story fit our recollections from Somalia, where the same group ran a "recreation program" that consisted of a semipro frisbee player from the United States who went to refugee camps giving out frisbees.

These people appeared at Wad Kowli a few days ago with seeds for the refugees going back to Tigre. They had it perfectly planned. Each refugee family going back to Tigre would get an individual bag of seeds. The seeds were already packaged in well-made bags of strong denim fabric.

But the seeds are too much extra weight. The refugees are on foot, already loaded down, and sometimes they must carry their children. REST offered to transport all the seeds into Tigre, when space becomes available on a truck, and to distribute the seeds there. Everyone advised giving the seeds to REST. The relief group insisted on distributing the seeds themselves, here at Wad Kowli, bag by bag, as originally planned.

Down the road a few kilometers, Martha found a huge pile of seeds lying in the dirt next to the road. All the different types of seeds were dumped together, waiting to rot. The refugees, unable to carry the extra weight, dumped out the seeds and kept the cloth bags.

May 15

Five patients have been admitted to the Médecins Sans Frontières hospital in shock with massive diarrhea. Rob Moodie, the MSF team leader, came by to get me. He held up a specimen container that was unmistakeable: thin gray watery fluid with stringy white flecks. Cholera has arrived.

We went back to the hospital, and I examined the patients and carefully checked their stories. They are not new arrivals, and they come from different parts of the camp. Then we sat down to decide how to start keeping track of the epidemic. We will have an emergency meeting tonight at 8:00 P.M.

In the meantime we visited Osman Mekki, and on our strong recommendation, he has agreed to close the camp. We are attempting to establish a quarantine. We called Gedaref by short-wave radio to alert Dr. Nabil, the Sudanese medical director of COR, and Dr. Richard Nesbit, the new medical advisor for UNHCR. They are scheduled to visit Wad Kowli tommorrow.

11:00 P.M.

The emergency meeting went well. Everyone is charged with adrenaline at the thought of this huge challenge.

We went step by step through the plan drafted several days ago. We had estimated a maximum of 750 serious cases over the first five days, with each serious case needing ten liters of IV fluids. We had listed, in detail, projected needs for antibiotics, IV sets, fluids, oral rehydration salts, sanitation supplies, even quicklime and shrouds. We also had a detailed plan of public health measures to control the disease and for tracking the source. Everything was now checked, discussed, and rechecked. Specific tasks were assigned.

The meeting was held under a three-sided thatch shelter at the UNHCR compound inside the camp. It lasted several hours, and by the time the meeting ended the camp was quiet.

We turned off the lanterns and were plunged into darkness. The spell of concentration was broken. It was drizzling, and the ground was already muddy. A wave of anxiety came over me. We still need supplies from the outside and daily water trucks. With heavy rain the roads will be impassable. We are not yet prepared.

May 16

Day 2 of the epidemic, and we recorded our first cholera death. At dawn some children found the body of a young woman in the defecation field on the edge of camp. Her family said she suddenly got very sick with vomiting and diarrhea late yesterday, and that last night she left her hut to go to the field. After a few hours they searched for her, but it was dark and she couldn't be found.

When we got into camp, we also discovered that the group of five or six thatch stalls next to Public Health Headquarters had been burned to the ground. So we have seen the first official cholera-control act of the Sudanese chief of sanitation: a torch to the place where expatriates buy coffee, Pepsi, and tea.

I hope the sanitarian has also arranged guards to keep people away from the stagnant pools in the riverbed. We suspect those pools are the source of the epidemic, and at the meeting last night we decided they should be rigidly off limits until they can be filled in.

We met with Nabil and Nesbit. Weeks ago they scheduled a visit to Wad Kowli to review plans and preparations for "001" (cholera). Now, when the visit actually happened, we not only described our plans, but told how they are working. It was a satisfying moment, but also laced with unreality and humor. At the top of Nabil's agenda was "control of visitors." This means journalists. He emphasized that "in the Sudan no one can release information about cholera except the president or prime minister." By chance, correspondents from the

New York Times and the London *Financial Times* are in camp this very moment. They are certain to file stories.

Nabil also insisted that we culture every single case. We asked him to bring culture containers when we radioed last night, and he brought five. We already have twenty-eight cases. Even if we had plenty of containers, it's impossible to do cultures without reliable electricity and a fully equipped lab. None of this exists at Wad Kowli or is likely to ever exist at Wad Kowli or anywhere nearby.

Rob Moodie missed the meeting with Nabil and Nesbit. He is sick with a violent headache and fever, and the MSF team asked if I would examine him. He has not been immunized for meningitis, and because of the severity of his headache and fever, I needed to do a spinal tap. The tap was normal. He has caught one of the severe viral illnesses endemic to this region. The infections, spread by mosquitoes, have exotic names such as dengue, Rift Valley fever, West Nile fever, O'nyong-nyong fever.

May 17

I went by the hospital and clinics to see how the cholera plans were working out. No problems with cholera, but at one of the clinics there was another medical-mistake story.

(opposite)
Outskirts of Wad Kowli refugee camp, May 18, 1985. A child begins the three-week journey on foot back to Tigre.

(page 194)
Outskirts of Wad Kowli refugee camp, May 18, 1985. Handing out clothes to a woman returning to Tigre.

The clinic had just ended, and the nurse was putting away the medicines when she noticed that a new container of the tranquilizer diazepam (Valium) was almost empty. Out of one thousand pills, perhaps nine hundred were gone. The container next to the tranquilizers was chloroquine, antimalaria pills. The chloroquine container was still full. Both pills are yellow and are the same size and shape. Apparently, the two containers got confused, and about one hundred malaria patients left clinic today with nine tranquilizers apiece instead of the nine antimalaria pills they were supposed to get.

And tonight again it rained—hard, steady, heavy tropical

rain. The soil is "black cotton"—a form of clay that doesn't drain. The ground in our compound has turned into deep sticky mud. Across the river there are forty thousand people under flimsy thatch shelters that were built for shade and will not keep out the rain. The tents that have been promised have not yet arrived. In my *tukul* I am completely dry, but I just got up to put on a sweater, because even under two blankets I was starting to get cold. The refugees are lying on the ground in this mud in the dark on the other side of the river. They are wet and cold. The night has just begun, and there is no way to get warm until morning. I can't imagine having little children who are in misery and knowing that nothing can be done to help them, nothing but wait for the sun that is ten hours away.

At least the one hundred malaria patients who got tranquilizers by mistake will get a good night's sleep.

May 18

This morning we found a 4-year-old girl walking on the road past our compound, looking for her parents. Somehow they had gotten separated, but she knew the destination was Sudan. The child didn't realize that she was already in Sudan, and we guessed that she thought Sudan was a village name, equivalent to her village in Tigre. In rags and all alone, she had crossed the riverbed and walked the mile from camp on her way to find them. We gave her food and a bath, and we bought some fabric for a new dress in the village. Then we took her back to camp to the REST compound, which functions as a lost and found center.

At dinner we learned that her father had found her. It was the event of the day for everyone.

May 19

The medical coordinator has been back several days. We have been working together and today I tried to tie up loose ends, because tomorrow I leave. I drafted a summary about repatriation for UNHCR in Gedaref and Khartoum. We are frustrated that the camp has still not been closed and concerned that cholera will rapidly spread all over eastern Sudan. (It did, but perhaps it would have spread no matter what.) We were able to halt evacuation of refugees from Wad Kowli to Ghirba, but not much else.

The trucks carrying refugees into Wad Kowli from other camps have continued to arrive. We tried to halt this movement, because refugees returning to Tigre might carry the epidemic back with them, spreading it widely as they return to different villages. We tried to quarantine the people in transit, but they have been leaving in the middle of the night. If the road is blocked they walk across the fields. It is impossible to stop them. My guess is that one-third to one-half of the refugees who come down with cholera during the trip home will die.

In late afternoon I visited the graveyard and took a long walk through the camp intending to take pictures. I saw a crazy man standing next to a fire despite the 110-degree heat, and four times I was accosted and led by the hand into different huts to see people who were sick. The first three were adults, not very sick, and after examining them I wrote a medication on their health card or on a piece of paper from my notebook and told them to go to the pharmacy in the morning. The people offered me tea. I sat for a few minutes with the families in their huts, enjoying the company even though we could not share words and made no effort to talk.

The fourth time was different. Just as it was getting dark, I was taken to see a child who was deathly ill. A beautiful but severely malnourished young girl, about 5 years old, was lying on the floor of the hut breathing far too rapidly. She was burning with fever and looked like she might not survive the night. How could this child have been missed?

There was nothing I could do but urge the father to take the girl to the hospital. I wrote a note to go with them. I could not give the father directions to the hospital, because, by that time, after wandering aimlessly in the huge camp, and with the darkness, I was lost. I left the hut feeling empty and incredibly sad. After all these months of effort, it seemed nothing had changed.

After walking a short while, I found where the big fire had been, and then I found the riverbed and my way home. I walked by the stagnant ponds, our possible cholera source. No guards were present, and refugees were using the water for bathing and washing clothes. ◊

May 21

I left Wad Kowli yesterday for Gedaref, and this morning I caught the UNHCR plane to Khartoum. I got a room at the Acropole Hotel, a good lunch, a nap, and a real bath, the first in almost three months.

Already I realize how fulfilling these past three months have been and that it will be impossible to explain Sudan when I get back home. My mind is filled with images from the camps.

I keep seeing the last patient I encountered, the 5-year-old girl who was burning with fever. The light had faded by the time I had examined her thin body. Early the next morning I led a group of refugee health workers, trying to find her hut. I had felt anxious when we found the burned area where the fire had been. I had been certain we were about to find her hut and filled with dread that we were too late. I still feel the frustration from our search. We never found her.

May 22

The Acropole Hotel swirls with rumor and activity. I met an Australian veterinarian who plans to go into Tigre with the TPLF to survey the livestock and determine what is needed to replenish their work animals. He also had several cases of video equipment, and he plans to make a movie. I met a Ph.D. candidate from Cornell University who is paid $150 a day as a consultant to organize a caravan of donkeys carrying seed grain into Tigre. He has three weeks for this, and I have heard that the desirable seed, teff, does not exist right now in any local or international market. I saw the *New York Times* reporter from Wad Kowli, who showed me the cholera story that he filed; and I had breakfast with a woman from New York City who is a reporter for the *Village Voice*.

I also got recent news about the Fau camps from a nurse I worked with in Somalia in 1981. She arrived as a volunteer a few weeks ago, caught malaria at Fau 3, and was evacuated to Khartoum. Another doctor in the Faus has caught hepatitis, and the snake count at Fau 3 is more than thirty. I heard stories about the new nutritionist at Fau 3, the woman I last saw on the bathroom floor in the guest house in Gedaref. A believer in "healing energies," she has been "laying on hands" with sick children in the feeding center and treating malnourished children with herbal teas.

May 24

I woke up at 2:00 A.M. dreaming about Wad Kowli. I could see hundreds of refugees, columns and columns streaming through what looked like a Sudanese village. People were banging on metal pots, and Martha was using Osman Mekki's short-wave radio to call for help.

In the morning I went to UNICEF and dropped off my film. I told the mission chief about the cholera outbreak. He asked if I would consider staying on in Sudan, as medical advisor to UNICEF. He wanted me to make a trip to the west, to Kordofan and Darfur.

I told him it was not possible. Tonight I leave Sudan.

(page 200)
Riverbed of the Atbara, Wad Kowli refugee camp, May 19, 1985. On my last afternoon in Wad Kowli, I wandered aimlessly through the camp, watching as refugees continued to use the deadly pond water for bathing and washing clothes.

Epilogue

TWO YEARS AFTER
Khartoum, Ghirba, Sefawa,
and Tukulubab,
March 3–April 15, 1987

(opposite)
Sefawa refugee camp, March 1987. The woman delivered her premature baby alone and cut the umbilical cord with a razor, but the baby bled to death because she didn't know to tie the cord first.

(page 204)
Ghirba refugee camp, March 1987. Camels cross the road as we drive out of camp.

March 3

It's now two years since the famine, and I sit in an empty Swissair jet, circling Khartoum airport waiting to land. I'm returning to survey for blindness and eye disease in the refugee camps, among the survivors, with hopes of learning how to manage better next time. I've brought a team of four, including two professors of ophthalmology. We will examine the children and adults who went blind from malnutrition, infection, and other reasons.

There are only five passengers in the huge plane. Everybody else got off in Cairo. I remember staring out the window as we circled Khartoum airport two years ago, wondering what I would find. The famine is over. There have been two years of excellent crops.

The hot African night air greets me as I get off the plane. While I'm still on the tarmac, half in the dark, I hear someone shout my name. After I fight my way through customs, I find Jessica Sanders, my colleague from Fau 3, who has come to meet me.

March 5

This evening we sat on the roof of Jessica's house, and she brought me up to date.

With the rainy season of 1985, Fau 3 was transformed. Health problems were controlled, and some months there was not a single death. Refugees from Fau 3 earned money harvesting the Sudanese crops and were able to open a market and tea houses. For the Sudanese farmers, the problems have radically changed. With two years of bumper crops, they face disastrously low prices and lack of storage space for the surplus.

The rains that came in the summer after I left gave the children of Fau 3 new activities. They made huge mudball "snowmen." They also made mud rectangles the size and shape of a radio and put a long straight stick in the top. After these creations had hardened in the sun, the children would hold them to their ears as they walked around camp, as if they were prowling a big city street.

Jessica tells me it will be impossible to do our eye survey at Fau 3. Only one thousand refugees still remain there. Some time in the next few weeks they will all be moved to Sefawa, and Fau 3 will close permanently.

March 11

I've spent the past week going back and forth between different camps, meeting the expatriate doctors and nurses, organizing survey and clinic sites, and recruiting staff. We will start at Ghirba, where Martha and I watched the first group of refugees arrive when the camp opened two years ago.

Today I met the British nurse we will work with. I found her in the Therapeutic Feeding Center putting a feeding tube into the stomach of a malnourished 7-month-old baby that weighed only twelve pounds. The child had a fever and was being treated for malaria, pneumonia, and tuberculosis. In the past two days the baby had gotten worse. The nurse asked me to review the case. I had nothing useful to add. The sense of déjà vu overwhelmed me, and I had to walk out of the room.

But this child is an exception. After two years, fewer than 5 percent of the children in the refugee camps are malnourished, and health in the camps is probably better than in the surrounding Sudanese villages. Everywhere there is vivid evidence of renewal and rebirth. It seems that almost every young woman has a new baby, or is pregnant, or both. Driving from one camp to the next, I notice that the camel herds are larger, and there are baby camels in every herd. I can not remember any babies two years ago.

March 14

Sefawa will be our second survey camp. It now houses all the refugees from Tigre who still remain in Sudan. In the last two days Fau 3 has been emptied. I drove into Sefawa just after the final truckload from Fau 3 had arrived. Two of the men from Fau 3 came over to greet me, remembering I was their doctor from two years ago.

Then a woman walked directly up to me. She stared as if she were seeing a ghost. From the way she looked, I had a terrible feeling that I'd cared for one of her children who did not survive.

April 15

Today, two years after it closed, we searched for the spot where Tukulubab had been. Tukulubab was the "death camp," the first stopping place for the refugees that I worked with at Fau 3.

We left Kassala and drove forty-five minutes over sandy tracks. Several times it looked like we might get stuck or that the track had ended. We repeatedly had to stop for directions. Some of the people did not know there had ever been a refugee camp in the area. At the base of Tukulubab rock, a man leading several camels knew of the camp, but he had no idea where it had been.

Fifty yards away we found a man quarrying rocks. He remembered. The refugee camp had been exactly where we were standing. Now, two years later, not a single stick or structure marked a city of forty thousand whose tragedy had filled the world press. The man pointed out where the COR office had been and directed us across to an opposing rock face to see the graves.

After a 15-minute walk we found sixty stone piles on the ground. I stared at the empty space between the two massive rock formations and tried to imagine the makeshift city that had disappeared. Eagles now soared near the top of the rock spire. It had become a single giant tombstone for a city that no longer lived. To the right of us, we looked out at the unmarked border of Ethiopia, trying to look out through time. A cycle of disaster had run its course and was being forgotten.

(page 210)
Graveyard, previous site of
Tukulubab refugee camp,
April 15, 1987.